MW01614128

LOVE GOD
AND
LEAVE THE LAST
DAYS BEHIND

PAUL RICHARD STRANGE SENIOR

Copyright © 2023 by Paul Richard Strange Senior

All rights reserved. This book or any portion thereof may not be reproduced
or transmitted in any form or manner, electronic or mechanical, including
photocopying, recording, or by any information storage or retrieval system,
without the express written permission of the copyright owner except for
the use of brief quotations in a book review or other noncommercial uses
permitted by copyright law.

Printed in the United States of America

Library of Congress Control Number: 2022922719
ISBN: Softcover   979-8-88622-845-8
           e-Book   979-8-88622-846-5

Republished by: PageTurner Press and Media LLC
Publication Date: 01/05/2023

To order copies of this book, contact:
PageTurner Press and Media
Phone: 1-888-447-9651
info@pageturner.us
www.pageturner.us

TABLE OF CONTENTS

INTRODUCTION TO LOVE GOD AND LEAVE THE LAST DAYS BEHIND

Much has been written about the general subject of Bible prophecy, especially in the last 100 years. So, why in the world should a Christian give the reading Christian public another book on this subject? This book represents a minority position in the body of Christ. From the earliest periods of the church fathers, the main views which have dominated modern Christian thinking have been present, in embryo form. None were fully developed. When Saint Augustine, Bishop of Hippo, wrote 'The City of God', his work solidified much of what today is called "amillenniallism", and his reputation enabled this view to be accepted in much of Christianity from the 5th Century to the present time! It was retained by most of the Protestant Reformers. For this reason, some scholars regard it as the most stable set of principles from which to resolve the myriad of issues that have to be answered for a coherent view.

Other views that are taught can also claim early church fathers for their positions. Ignatius and Papias and Tertullian, for example, advocated a literal 1000 years of Christ reigning with His saints, as we learn about in the 20th Chapter of the Book of the Revelation of Jesus Christ as Conquering King. Origen voiced a profound Gospel optimism that some could see as an early version of what is today called "post-millenniallism", which anticipates that Christ will return to a fully Christianized world.

Besides these three views, another one is built upon the fact that Jesus Christ foretold the war between Jerusalem and Rome about 40 years before it occurred. Most theologians acknowledge that this was an amazing fulfillment of Christ's words, documented by secular historians Josephus and Tacitus. Yet, the controversy among Christians has to do with the implications of this First Century fulfillment upon the course of history and the effect upon other Christian teachings, such as the resurrection of the dead, the final judgment, and the nature of the afterlife.

The big question is really, "what is the best definition of the Biblical term 'last days'"? Did Jesus really tell His disciples that human civilization and the planet was going to come to an end? Many say "yes", but I say "no, not at all!" Jesus taught that the "world" would end, but He wasn't talking about the rocks and hills and solar system. He was talking about an Age, which is how the same word is translated now in most translations. An age would close in its last days.

Christians agree that the Biblical last days began in the events of the First Century. The Apostle Peter told his audience who observed the first outpouring of the Holy Spirit at Pentecost that they were witnessing a fulfillment of the words of the ancient Hebrew Prophet Joel, which was given for the last days. There are too many verses for any Bible reader to deny which tell us that the days when the Apostles of Christ were preaching and teaching were the last days.

But, the First Century was only the "first days" of the New Covenant in Jesus Christ, not its last days. So, what was the First Century the last days of? This book will seek to carefully present the case that the last days of the Old Covenant worship system, centered around animal sacrifices in the physical City of First Century Jerusalem, was fully replaced by the true permanent Temple of God, the Christian Church among all nations, where believers gather to offer spiritual sacrifices of thanksgiving and praise. Just as our Lord told the Woman at the Well, the time was due when neither Jerusalem, nor a mountain, was "the place" to worship God, it would be wherever people gathered to worship Him in spirit and in truth.

MY CONFESSION OF CHRISTIAN CONVICTIONS

People who write about spiritual subjects from the point of view of claiming to believe in the Bible, and to be followers of God through His Son Jesus Christ, do well to elaborate on the basic convictions that motivate them. Are we Pentecostal or Charismatic? Are we Calvinistic or non-Calvinistic? Are we believers in immersion only or do we also allow for the baptism of little people to be valid? While these issues do not determine the sum total of any Christian's credibility by any stretch, they help the reader who cares about the writer's starting point within Christian thinking. So, here goes for me:

I, Paul Richard Strange, Senior, believe that the sacred writings accepted by Protestant Christians as the 39 books of the Old Testament and the 27 books of the New Testament are specially inspired by God in His own unique way, so that we have every reason to fully rely upon these writings as accurate, able to teach us, correct us, and revise our views on all subjects. I do not believe that God gave to His people the inspired words in these holy books for us to learn about gravity, nor the technical aspects of how our universe works. Rather, we are given the Word of God to help us know our Creator, Redeemer, and Ruler and to understand His marvelous covenant with all Who are His! While I share the Protestant view of the Apocrypha as not inspired, like the Bible, I think they contribute much positive value to Christianity;

I believe that the only way that the Old Testament can be rightly discerned is through the teachings of the Lord Jesus and His Holy Apostles, via the New Testament Scriptures, which fulfill and explain

3

the Old Testament Scriptures, and that Jesus Christ Himself is the Great Theme of the whole of Scripture;

I believe that God saves sinners by His own sovereign grace alone, through His free gift of faith in His Son Jesus Christ, and that true faith always produces good works of obedience, motivated by love;

I believe that God sent His Son Jesus Christ into the world to save sinners, that our Lord Jesus came as God with us, Who took on flesh without ever sinning, was born of the Virgin Mary, lived a sinless life, worked real miracles in the sight of the people as He taught the people, was crucified under Pontius Pilate, rose up bodily from the realm of the dead. He also proved Himself by many infallible proofs to be the Son of God, ordained His apostles to proclaim Him and plant churches throughout all of the known world, judged the City of Jerusalem in 70 A.D., and this ended forever the Old Covenant system of animal sacrifices and rituals that were no longer valid after His saving death and glorious resurrection. He is Lord of lords, King of kings, and the Final Judge of every one of us, to Whom we shall all one day give an account. He is the only Savior of sinners, by Whose Name Alone forgiveness is received by persons in all nations, all languages, all generations, and Who has transformed our world, both now and forever.

On some matters where Christians disagree, I respectfully hold to the following without being dogmatic: that the signs and miracles and wonders that occurred during the First Century were given to speak to the Nation of Israel in her last days, and to authenticate the Apostles of our Lord Jesus Christ, and were not intended by the Holy Spirit to be generally part of the Christian message or practice in all of the many generations since the Apostles went to be with the Lord. To me, the fact that all Christians are the sons and daughters of Abraham is an excellent reason to embrace with joy the baptizing of not only those who come to faith in Jesus, but also, little people born to practicing Christian households. Since the Holy Spirit was "poured out" upon the believers in the Book of Acts, and this was called the "baptism of or with the Holy Spirit", I do not believe that Christians are bound to only one mode of baptizing. Since the baptism of the Spirit placed believers of Jewish heritage and non-Jewish heritage together into Christ and His body, this would mean that the spiritual result could be viewed as an immersion, as well. For these reasons, the uniqueness of the practice of baptizing during the time when the Apostles were leading and teaching the churches, and appointing Christian bishops where churches were planted, is not something dogmatic. There is liberty for both baptistic and non-baptistic Christian understandings, in my humble opinion. I realize that many Christians have a different view. The continuing Christians since the end of the Jewish Age in 70 A.D. have always baptized in all places where believers come together together to form communities for worship, covenant faithfulness, teaching, outreach to the poor, and mutual encouragement. This is sufficient reason to respect each church's right to some variation in practice.

Christianity is the true Israel of God. God took the remnant of Old Covenant Israel in the First Century, those who believed the Gospel and were baptized into Christ and His kingdom, and united them with the Gentiles who came to Christ by believing the Gospel. Together, they became one new man, the Church among all nations, the Wife of the Lamb, the Israel of God, and the family of God in heaven and earth eternally united in Jesus Christ. The modern European Israelis are our neighbors who we are to love and care about as we do our neighbors of every other non-Christian persuasion. They are not Biblical Israel.

All who believe that Jesus Christ is the Son of God from the heart, and who love God and people, are born from above spiritually. They are sons and daughters of the ancient Patriarch Abraham. In baptism, God claims them for Himself, as this is the covenant sign of the friendship between God and Abraham, just as male circumcision was the sign and seal of the covenant in the centuries from Abraham to the salvation achieved for believers at the Cross of Christ.

All of these convictions would probably define me as a covenantalist, an evangelical in classical terms, and a preterist, which is a term that means that most or all of the prophesied events are in the past.

There are divisions among preterist Christians about how much of the whole of prophecy is behind us. Some pick out a few events and make them unfulfilled, in order to be at peace with the hyper-popular futurism of modern American culture. I cannot do that, even though I am not convinced that it is necessary to defend a label. Since I believe that the ongoing Christian Church among all nations is most definitely an outworking of the fulfillment of Bible prophecy, and that the ongoing kingdom of God is always "fulfilling" its mission, this would seem to imply something less than total past fulfillment.

Here is how I would attempt to explain this issue of full or partial preterism. We do not believe, as Christians, that God is giving forth inspired writings beyond the canon accepted already. We believe that the foundation of trying to be obedient to God is the complete and final authority of Scripture. There are all kinds of debates about the weight of tradition, councils, and arising spiritual movements within Christianity, as well as reason and debate, as to how much it should effect our INTERPRETATION of Scripture. After all, a unified interpretation of difficult areas of the Bible has never been easy in any generation of the Faith in Jesus! So it is that we can believe that we have the complete and final written revelation of God in the Bible, in contrast to cults which rely upon extra-Biblical material for their worship and teaching, without believing that any individual Christian is able to independently get all of the interpretation of the Scriptures fully correct. Inspiration does not include infallibility of interpretation among any tradition of Christianity. We all really need each other, working diligently, to get it right!

I am open to all criticisms and other feedback. Write me at:

Paul Richard Strange Senior
119 Marvin Gardens
Waxahachie Texas 75165
I'll respond if at all possible in a timely manner.
    In the King of kings, Paul

WHY THINK ABOUT THE BIBLICAL LAST DAYS?

There is nothing that any of us can actually do that will change the destiny of mankind, as far as what God has determined in eternity as the length of generations for human history to continue. Therefore, why should anyone pay very much attention to the subject of the Biblical last days? That is the mind frame of more than a few people alive. Others are fascinated with efforts to read current events and fit them into a narrative, mixed together with selective general Biblical predictions, and try to assure themselves that the end of the world is at hand. Persons who love God and love people have more important reasons to think about the Biblical last days than either curiosity nor sensationalism! All who love God and people, especially persons who confess that Jesus Christ truly is Lord over all of life and history and the future, are thinking about a subject that defines the very credibility of Christ Himself!

We who confess the faith that is in Jesus, whether we come from older or more recent Christian organizational affiliations, share in common many things. Even though we have more than a few differences of opinion, the common confession that God sent Jesus to be the true Savior binds us. Among the many roles of Christ such as Shepherd, Bread of Life, Hope of Israel, Seed of the Woman, Seed of Abraham, Son of David, and Priest after the Order of Melchizedec, is included the role of the Last Prophet from God. This is a claim that is made by Islam for Muhammed, but Christians deny that any true Prophet of any new message came since Jesus. If our claim is well founded, then it cannot be discovered that Jesus made any errors in His role as the Prophet of God.

Some Christians have joined atheists in claiming that Jesus made a major prophetic mistake. The prolific and popular writer of Christian novels, C.S. Lewis, made this claim. He felt it was very embarrassing that Jesus promised to come back in the natural lifetime of some of His First Century followers, because He failed to do so. The mantra of both anti-Christian philosophers and Christian thinkers has been that the Lord Jesus did not come back when He told His First Century disciples that He would return. For many Christians, when they permit themselves to pay at least minimal attention to the Bible passages which clearly indicate that the coming of the Son of Man would occur in the First Century, their first instinct is to say that these inspired words cannot mean what they seem to mean.

So, why should every single Christian think seriously about the Biblical last days? Because, our hope in Christ rests upon His verifiable integrity, not only because of the case for His resurrection from the dead, for His miracles during His ministry, and for the amazing number of messianic expectations that have been fulfilled by His visit, starting in His birth in Bethlehem, but also, because He foretold the end of the world. He spoke with authority as the Son of God telling His followers specific things about how the world (or "age") that they were then living in would close out. If He was mistaken, then it would seem that the critics of the Christian Faith are right. Yet, if He was correct about everything, then everyone has a strong reason to give more than a casual examination of the words related to the Biblical last days!

If those of us who insist that the Biblical last days both began and also ended in the events of the first generation after the Lord arose out from the dead are on the right track, then movies like the 'Leftbehind Series' should be judged as mere entertainment with zero foundation for any solid Christian to formulate a serious view of the Biblical last days. If we who see the Biblical last days as completed are mistaken, then it is the moral duty of sincere Christians to do more than rail against us on the basis of comfortable creedalism. If honorable, they will prove from Scripture in very plain terms why we are not correct!

THE LAST DAYS OF WHAT?

I grew up believing with all of my heart that we were living in the last days of human history as we know it. Almost everybody that I knew in church life also was certain that Christ's Second Coming was very, very close to taking place. When I was thirteen, I remember sneaking outside at night several times due to being awake wondering if I might be able to directly witness this event. It didn't happen, but I sure wanted it to happen! That would have been the coolest thing to be imagined. It would have solved some problems for me, but it seemed that it caused some other problems. If I was ready and not actively doing anything wrong, it would save me from a whole of lot of serious mistakes, for sure. On the other hand, I had dreams about life that made me kind of hope that the Second Coming could hold off a little while.

My youthful immaturity is somewhat humorous to me now, but it doesn't change certain questions and difficulties that many people have about what seems like a Christian jigsaw puzzle, that is, the diverse opinions about the Second Coming of Christ, based in part upon how we read the Biblical phrase "last days". Are there any clues in the New Testament Scriptures about how to rightly interpret the term "last days"? Or, is it up to your prerogative or mine as a matter of flipping a spiritual coin? Are there any solid principles relevant to coming to a strong certainty about exactly what the Lord Jesus and the holy Apostles meant by the last days? What questions can we ask to help us get the right answers?

One question that seems to this writer to be begging for all Christians to ask is, "the Biblical last days were or are the last days of what?" I am so surprised that it is nearly impossible to prompt any Christian to ask this question! But, doesn't it seem to be very pertinent to caring at all about what Jesus taught? Personally, I strongly suspect that millions of Christians are unwilling to think about this question because they know that one of the possible answers will be unpopular in church. Nevertheless, let us explore the two main possible answers to the question, "the Biblical last days were or are the last days of what?" In church history, some have said it was the end of the Old Covenant Age with its full replacement with the New Covenant Age. The other view is that it means the last days of history.

Christians from a wide variety of views already agree that the last days began in the First Century. This is a pretty good place to start. When the Holy Spirit was poured out upon the disciples gathered in Jerusalem on the Day of Pentecost, as explained in the 2nd Chapter of the Book of the Acts of the Apostles, a conversation started. Some observers of this amazing phenomena suggested that the disciples were drunk. The Apostle Peter stood and preached to the Jews gathered from many places and told them that these people were not drunk, but were experiencing something that their ancient Hebrew Prophet Joel had foretold would occur in the last days. This is only one of many examples of references to the last days as being the days of the Apostles that can be offered. The Apostle Paul wrote to the Christians in First Century Corinth and told them in Chapter 10 and verse 11 that their generation was the one to whom the ends of the ages had come. So it is that hardly any reputable Christian denies the beginning of the Biblical last days in the First Century. But, they still manage to stretch the last days out to our very day!

The first generation of New Covenant followers of God through Jesus Christ were living in the last days of something, but it certainly was not the last days of the New Covenant transformation of all things! Truly, the days of the ministry of the Apostles were the "first days" of the Christian Church in the whole world, and people confessing and believing in Christ's death, burial and resurrection. It was only the start of the New Covenant, which has continued for nearly twenty centuries since. Yet, in spite of this, more than a few scholars and ministers insist to Christians and observers that we are presently living in the last days. This is because, while they admit that the last days began in the First Century, they cannot admit that the last days ended also in the First Century. So it is that we have a set of last days that is like that never ending song that never ends because it never ends without ending (okay, you get the point.)

What are the reasons why so few church leaders can admit that the last days ended in the First Century? We know some factors, although probably not all. Theological reasons exist, emotional reasons exist, and financial reasons exist. No doubt there are others, but these three deserve some attention.

People who want to be faithful to the statements of the historic Christian creeds often assume that it is virtually impossible that the creeds could be severely mistaken. Since they consider it a severe mistake to admit that the last days ended in the First Century, due to the idea that the end of the last days requires the Second Coming of Christ, they are, therefore, locked into denying that the last days ended. To them, to admit that the last days ended in the First Century is tantamount to admitting that the Christian majority has been severely mistaken on an issue essential to the proper definition of the New Covenant Christian Faith. Therefore, they have placed their minds off limits to any information, including plain Bible statements, that seem to present the case that the last days are gone, bye-bye, and way behind us!

Emotional factors also compel more than a few Christians to be completely disinterested in knowing in their hearts whether or not the popular view of the everlasting last days is correct. It tends to effect how people view you socially if you stubbornly insist on something just because it's right. That is often a source of tremendous and impractical annoyance. For these folks, social propriety requires of all of us that we almost never fail to go with the popular flow on any issue, at least, until the elite give a thumbs up!

Financial reasons compel a lust for the popular view of Bible prophecy, as there is a market for the dramatic and sensational. If Christians were to become addicted to serious Bible study, and challenge the popular opium of finding 666 in every new prominent public figure and/or license plate, some gurus of some very weird prophecy teachings would stand to lose a fortune!

There was something that was growing old and about to

completely pass away forever during the days of the ministry of the Apostles. At the Cross, according to Christians, Jesus became the One Sacrifice for sin forever to all persons in all places, languages, races, nations, and generations who would ever trust in His Name, call upon Him, confess Him as Lord, and be His disciple. So, the continuation of animal sacrifices served out there purpose. They had no validity of any kind once the Perfect Lamb of God was offered for the sins of mankind. This brought about a showdown between the Gospel as preached by the Apostles, and the guardians of the Temple, who saw themselves as permanent. They could not conceive that it was possibly Yahweh's will to replace the Temple in Jerusalem with a spiritual Temple, the Body of Christ.

The war that ended the Jewish temple sacrifices in the City of First Century Jerusalem was a major fulfillment of the words of Jesus. Also, it brought something to a close in its last days. When we ask ourselves, "The Biblical last days were the last days of what?", the answer that makes the most sense is the thing that actually ended in the First Century, according to history. We should ask ourselves questions, from time to time, that our outside of our normal comfort zones. This is one we should ask.

✝

ALL CHRISTIANS
ARE COVENANT KIDS

PAUL RICHARD STRANGE, SR   dadprs@hotmail.com

Jesus Christ connected all of the remnant church from the Twelve Tribes of Israel, to all of the persons given to Him by the Father from among the non-Jewish nations, and they formed together His church, which took place in the First Century A.D. This is the outworking of God's covenant with Abraham, which is now presented to mankind in fulfilled terms. The New Covenant Christian Church is for people in all nations and ages who call on the Name of the Lord Jesus with a heart purified by faith in His saving death and glorious resurrection. We all belong to each other, we all share in the common salvation, and we are all covenant kids. The New Covenant really is a covenant, with real covenant blessings for obedience and real covenant curses for disobedience.

It is my conviction that Christianity finds its healthiest expressions in the lives of families and churches and societies whenever a high percentage of believers in all types of churches reason from a more covenantal mindset. The covenantal mindset, beginning with the realization that Christians are Abraham's descendants, leads us differently about some matters than if we neglect to preach and teach that Christians are Abraham's descendants.

Many Christians bring little children to the church to receive water baptism, which identifies a child born to Christian parents as a descendant of Abraham. Large numbers of Christian families bring little children to receive a special prayer of dedication to the Lord. While I agree with the practice of baptizing little ones born to practicing Christians, it is a joyful reality that Christians instinctively have a keen interest in the spiritual lives of little ones. This is, I believe, a covenantal instinct.

Covenantal thinking reflects itself in many other ways in Christian congregations, as well. The breaking of the Bread and drinking of the Cup in the communion of Christ's body and Christ's blood is a testimony that all believers partake of Christ together, share an eternal family connection, and enjoy the celebration of the defeat of sin and death at the Cross.

Since all Christians are covenant kids, it behooves us to affirm the things which are most reflective of our covenantal connection to Jesus Christ and to all fellow Christians of all generations, past, present and future. The first part of grabbing hold of what it means to be covenant kids is to preach and teach more faithfully and frequently that Jesus Christ is the Seed of Abraham, through Whom God has fulfilled His promises to the ancient Patriarch Abraham, and that Christians are the New Jerusalem Wife of the Lamb, and the Holy Temple of God.

Two physical "seeds" come out of Abraham: Isaac and Ishmael. Both of these descendants of Abraham became great nations. But, even greater is the fact that through faith in Jesus Christ, an innumerable multitude have been made into children of Abraham, justified by faith as Abraham was justified, and accepted by grace into the kingdom of Jesus Christ with no relevance of language, nationality or any other natural distinction! The hesitancy of some pastors to make it plain that Christians are Abraham's descendants is a hindrance to a more joyful covenant life in our churches. May we change this, for God's glory. All Christians are covenant kids!

BIBLE INTERPRETATION FOR ORDINARY CHRISTIAN READERS

The Protestant Bible contains 39 books of the Old Testament and 27 books of the New Testament. There are apocryphal books included in the Bibles recognized by the Roman Catholic Church and the Orthodox Church. The Apocryphal writings contain very helpful history, but are not universally accepted as part of the canon of Scripture. Among the books regarded by Christians as given by inspiration of God, much of it is written in narrative language that most of us can get a handle on. Other parts are written in styles that are not part of the straightforward language of everyday speech, and require more diligent effort. For these reasons, those of us who are ordinary believers in God through Christ who desire to be the best Bible students that we can possibly be do well to follow some basic interpretation guidelines that have been beneficial to large numbers of Christians over many centuries.

One plan is to examine any Bible book we are studying with an intent to seek to lay hold on the most clear passages as our first priority. For example, if there is one thing that is pretty clear about the very title of Genesis, it is that the word means "beginnings". Beginnings are going to be discussed. We may find that people have strong differences of opinion, for example, about whether the first chapter is talking about the actual history of the natural universe and the planet we live on, or else, is more about the beginning of the covenant connection between the Creator, Redeemer and Ruler and His people. But, we have a clear marker in the fact that beginnings are significant factors in this work. That gives us a standard of measurement which can help us to understand what all that the Creator began to do.

Another factor that is worth keeping in mind, for the Christian student of the Bible, is the importance of covenant as a great theme of the unfolding of the Bible. We can see this happening early in the fact that the woman is promised that her seed would crush the head of the serpent in the third chapter of Genesis. This cannot seriously be understood as a prediction that humans have been destined to go around stepping on the heads of literal snakes! Rather, it is an indicator of the truth taught by the Lord Jesus, when He told His followers and the Jews, "You search the Scriptures, because you think that in them you have eternal life; and it is they that bear witness about Me." (John 5:39) So it is that another sound principle for all Christian Bible readers is to expect to find Christ in the whole Bible.

There are passages that are meant to be more difficult and to require more work for us to come to a solid understanding. If we compare language usage, we are better equipped to allow the Bible to interpret itself, and avoid some of the errors of reading our own natural human instincts into the text. An example of this is when the Scriptures speak of wrath coming upon a specific ancient society, such as Sodom and Gomorrah, ancient Babylon, or ancient Egypt, for example. Especially, in Isaiah's prophecy of the destruction of Babylon in the 13th Chapter of that Old Testament book, a pattern can be seen. The ancient Hebrew Prophet speaks of the sun, moon, and stars ceasing to function. He also speaks of the Lord mustering an army from "the ends of the heavens". In this judgment, God promises to "punish the world for its evil and the wicked for her sins", even though it is only one great ancient city being punished. The earth is said to be removed out of its place. We can understand the fierceness of this use of language to describe the horrors of a major war that wipes out a civilization only if we know that it is not intended to be read as literal language. The sun, moon, and stars still function, as they were important parts of speech to communicate the seriousness of a war that is documented in human history!

When we come to the events of the time of the end in the New Testament, every Christian Bible reader ought to keep in mind the way that the destruction of Babylon was described by Isaiah. In the tradition of the ancient Hebrew prophets, our Lord Jesus Christ used very, very similar language to describe the end of the world, as recorded in the parallel accounts of Matthew 24, Mark 13, and Luke 21. Jesus spoke of the sun, moon and stars ceasing to function as He taught His disciples about the end of the world that would take place in their natural lifetime. Some of them would live to see their beloved capitol City of Jerusalem destroyed by foreign armies. The temple that they were admiring would be utterly destroyed and leveled to the ground. The small minority of Jews surviving that horrible period of tribulation would be gathered and sold into slavery to the surrounding nations, and the City of First Century Jerusalem would be burned. Yet, the picture in some of our English translations is that of the end of the world in general, instead of "age", as the Greek work means. This has led millions of modern Christians to insist that this as a tribulation for modern times, even though Jesus said it was a once only event. If we apply the standard of relying on the way in which prophetic language was used by Isaiah regarding the final destruction of Babylon, we will not need to be confused by the same language describing the end of the Jewish Temple Age with the destruction of the City and the Temple after a three and one-half year siege.

Allowing statements that are most clear to help us read and interpret statements that are less clear has been spoken of by many Christians as a great tool that we should take advantage of. This does not require that we obtain specialized training in theology, although that is a helpful tool, if possible. We simply start to seek out the clearest portions of the Bible book we are reading to help us grab hold of the general direction that the writer, inspired by the Holy Spirit, is taking us to see and learn.

Another example of applying this approach to the study of the last days, just as we can apply it to all other areas of coming to enjoy the whole of Scripture, is found in how we invest time in a reading that most Christians have found very complicated. More than a few Bible commentators have decided to stay away from the complications involved in discerning the images and symbols and eerie pictures presented in the Revelation of Jesus Christ written by John on the Isle of Patmos for the seven churches in Asia Minor (modern Turkey). The visions of heavenly scenes, bowls of wrath, terms like "Mystery Babylon", beasts, the number 666, the two witnesses, as well as lampstands can be thoroughly confusing. However, even in the investigation of this work that has so much apocalyptic symbolism, there is given to the reader a foundation of clear help. In the opening verses of introduction, in very clear and plain language, the reader is told that the events to be described are things which must "shortly come to pass", and reinforced with the words "for the time is near". In the 22nd and last chapter of the Revelation (or "unveiling") of Christ as Conquering King over all nations, Jesus says five times that He is coming soon. In verse 12, He tells the original readers that His reward is with Him. So, we can know that, even if we have to do a great deal of work to come to grips with how it all fits together, that this was written to encourage early Christians in the sufferings and persecutions that they were experiencing at that time, as the main and primary spiritual purpose, secondary to revealing the glorious Kingship of Jesus! The spectacular events given to the reader in symbolic terms unfolded shortly after John received these visions, wrote them down, and sent them to the seven churches listed in chapters 2 and 3.

The point here is that we are not without help in our goal of becoming good Christian Bible readers who please God and avoid the errors of sensationalism, on one extreme, or else, skeptical distance from a vigorous pursuit of the whole of the Scriptures, on the other. We can recognize that God has used every form of speech style to speak to His creation, especially, those who are His through faith in His Son. While not all of the Bible was intended to be easy to understand, much of it is. Our responsibility to ourselves is to go beyond just becoming Christian debate experts, and truly enjoy the Word of God, for ourselves, our children, and our grandchildren. Thanks be to God!

THE IMPLICATIONS OF WORDS

It is my opinion that we human beings who love the Lord Jesus and His people and His word have sometimes made some of the Bible more confusing than it should be. I do not believe that this is something we have done intentionally. From the perspective of the descriptions in the Bible of how the Fall of Man has effected every part of our lives, including our discernment of Biblical language, it is not even all that surprising. So, it is not in a condemning attitude that I challenge the prevailing opinions about the key issues related to Bible prophecy. It is due to a strong belief that we can do better if we appreciate and respect the implications of words that the Holy Spirit inspired the authors to write. As we make an effort to compare language usage with language usage, we come closer to seeing the Bible interpret the Bible, rather than simply my opinion, or that of John Doe down the street.

What are the implications of the words that tell us that Jesus spoke of events that would be fulfilled in the generation alive when He appeared as the Final Voice from heaven to teach His people about the unfolding of the kingdom of God among men? It seems that a departure from a solid understanding of the events that were foretold by the ancient Hebrew Prophet Daniel took place early in church history. This is an important consideration. In order to discern the most accurate way to read the Book of Daniel, it is vital for Christians to understand how deviations from sound words cause generations of confusion.

Two early Christian leaders first spoke of a break between the 69th and 70th week foretold by Daniel. It was well accepted among Christians prior to this that the 70 weeks that Daniel was told about in visions for his people, the Jewish Nation, were fulfilled when the Romans invaded

Jerusalem and destroyed the Temple. This is very important. Iranaeus and Hippolytus were the first Christian teachers to deviate from that well received view which is so important to the realization that the Jewish Age ended the Biblical last days, and fully empowered the New Covenant Age which is everlasting and has no end.

Clement of Alexandria and Origen of Alexander and Tertullian all taught that the 70th week of Daniel's prophecy was concluded by the final invasion of First Century Jerusalem. This was also the report of Bishop Athanasius who served in Alexandria for fifty years from 326 a.d. to 376 a.d. These were powerful witnesses of the complete fulfillment of the Jewish Age and the foundation for what should have been the norm in Christian thinking about the distinction of the Christian Age which followed the destruction of Jerusalem in 70 a.d. Of course, it is true that the two ages overlapped, and that has lent some confusion to Christians. Many expositors insist that the Age when the Apostles were preaching and gathering souls into the church has continued, and that we are still in what the Apostles would have called "this present evil age". The pervasiveness of that approach is due to the fact that we are often compelled to pay little attention to the logical implications of the Word of God! An error in regard to how we understand the end of the world of the Jewish Age confuses Christians enormously! It forces us to deny that the fullness of the Christian Age manifestation of the kingdom of God has come in, and this limits our thinking severely. The implications of rejecting the newness of the Christian Age and its everlasting blessings for all of humanity are something that we should pray and work to correct.

The implications of any willingness to admit that the Fall of Jerusalem was a major fulfillment of Bible prophecy is too important for any serious Christian Bible student to ignore. If we admit that Jesus Christ told the truth when He foretold the destruction of First Century Jerusalem, and this major fulfillment of Bible prophecy brought about the 70 weeks foretold by the ancient Hebrew Prophet Daniel, then we must re-order our Christian thinking in line with the Bible. Instead, we are often inclined to rationalize things that cannot be fit any better than a round object in a square peg. For example, if we realize that Daniel's prophecy came to pass in 70 a.d., and the final judgment upon national and ethnic Israel took place, then we can also recognize that the Christian Church is the true Israel for all generations! It is not such a stretch at all. God ingrafted formerly Gentiles into Israel, through the manifestation of the church in the world. Together, the remnant from the last days of Old Covenant Israel united with the many given to Christ from among the non-Jewish nations, and they became one new man forever, the church, the New Jerusalem, the Temple of the Holy Spirit, the eternal people of God, the Israel of God.

False teachers in modern times took the ancient error of Iranaeus and Hippolytus, denying the fulfillment of Daniel's 70 weeks in the First Century, and have caused many millions of people to doubt that believers in Jesus Christ are the true daughters and sons of Father Abraham. Instead, they believe that modern Zionists are the truly chosen ones, and that the church is some sort of very secondary consideration in the eyes of God Almighty. This deprives Christians of the spiritual wealth of their heritage, even though not all who generally embrace this false teaching realize its effects, and many are not fanatical. Nevertheless, God is raising up Christians who are not falling for this error, and who want the blessings of God's covenant in Christ to be more meaningful and real to all of our covenant family and friends, for the glory of God, and for the churches to flourish in the years to come, rather than fearfully hoping for salvation from the world in a sudden removal of all Christians off the planet.

The consensus of the majority of the early church fathers was true, which was that Daniel's 70 weeks were completed in the Jewish and Roman War. But, the implications of those words were not yet made clear to very many Christians. The lack of meditation upon WHY words matter to Christians has an effect of leaving us wide open to the kinds of fascinating novels that tickle the ears and entertain us, like the book 'The Late Great Planet Earth' by Hal Lindsey, or the 'Leftbehind Series' of novels and movies. We have become an evangelical church culture that can barely gather for worship to our God through Christ without a band to entertain us these days in the United States of America! We study religious marketing more than we care about the substance of approaching the Holy! This infantile craving upon Christian church culture probably is no accident. Here, I am NOT condemning persons who praise God differently than the liturgies of Christianity, Protestant and otherwise, for all previous centuries. Rather, it is the social rejection and intolerance of anything perceived to the human emotions as "boring" that is a problem. Why is this? Because it tends to make it a social sin to worship God with the mind, and to recognize that the coming together of the covenant community should be about God through Christ as the Guest of Honor, rather than more about how we feel at the sense level.

It is nearly impossible in much of modern evangelical Christian church life (or in much of the more liturgical church community, for that matter), to seriously engage in a reasonable discussion of Bible passages about the fulfillment of the Scriptures in the events of the First Century. It is not as though there are not plenty of such Bible passages. Even if you read the works of people who teach futurism, many will admit that the Apostles expected the return of Christ in their times. So, what happened? Did Jesus Christ make a mistake? Of course not! All true Christians agree that Christ the Son of God is perfect, and flawless, and incapable of error. What has simply happened has been that generations of Christ's people have ignored the implications of inspired words. That is the challenge for all who love the Lord in all generations and in all places and in all languages. When we take the time to examine the implications of Bible words, even when it involves issues that make us not so comfy, we are blessed!

✝

THIS GENERATION

The words "this generation" appear in many key passages in the New Testament Scriptures. There was something unique about the generation of Jewish people alive when the Son of God came in the flesh to visit man. The culture of the leaders of the Nation of Israel, struggling to keep some semblance of being a free people, even though depending upon relationships with the authorities of the Roman Caesar to maintain power, had a fine line to walk. They were a generation of leaders who had to be political and to preserve their positions of authority both in religion and in society. This is why they could not tolerate the rise of the disciples of Jesus. They instinctively sensed that their standing with Rome was in jeopardy if too many people came to regard this Jesus as the long-awaited Messiah of the Old Testament prophets. As a generation, they were predisposed to write off ANY claim that they did not control.

Jesus called them an "evil generation" on several occasions. In one instance, the Jewish leaders asked Jesus for a miraculous sign (see Matthew 12: 35-39). Jesus told them that an "evil and adulterous generation" seeks a sign. He called them evil and adulterous, in the sense of spiritual betrayal of their covenant with God, and one of the evidences was that they wanted to see a miracle on demand. This is interesting, in part, because Jesus did perform signs and wonders. Also, after His death and raising out from the dead, He empowered His apostles to do many signs and wonders. Jesus was obviously not opposed to doing works that were only explainable by Supernatural intervention into natural human daily life. But, He rebuked as sinister the craving for a show of miracles, as some sort of theatrical performance, designed to merely impress the immediate imagination, rather than very a message. An elaboration of this discussion takes place in the early verses of Matthew, Chapter 16. Jesus was not about to do miracles on demand merely for a show to fascinate the natural human senses.

Jesus condemned the generation alive when He came in the flesh also because of their particular level of hardness of heart. (see Matthew 12: 41-45). He taught that the men of Ninevah would rise to condemn the generation of First Century Jews. He also said that the Queen of the South would condemn that particular generation. He was pointing out that the people alive to be referred to as "this generation" during His visit in the flesh had achieved a degree of coldness and hardness that was incorrigible.

Jesus listed many hypocrisies of the Jewish leaders in Matthew 23 that was brining upon themselves and the entire nation the special wrath of God. They were guilty in that generation of the First Century of being only outwardly holy, of laying heavy burdens on the people, of doing good deeds to be seen of men, and of exaggerating their religious garb to impress each other, as well as enjoy the most prestigious seats in the banquet halls. Status was much more important than mercy and justice. For these and other reasons listed, Jesus told pronounced judgment upon "this generation" living at that time. They were living in the last generation of the Nation of Israel as constituted under Moses.

So, by the time the reader of the Gospel according to Matthew comes to Chapter 24, verse 34, it is in keeping with Christ's teachings in earlier settings. During this discussion with His disciples upon the Mount of Olives, they praise the beautiful Temple of Solomon. Rather than reinforcing their pride and delight in the central most important Jewish expression of their religion and heritage, Jesus told them that everything that they were looking at would be utterly destroyed. They were taken aback and asked when this would happen and what would be the sign of His coming. His answer was, "this generation shall not pass away until all of these things take place."

WHY I BELIEVE IN THE CHRISTIAN TEACHING OF THE TRINITY

One of the main reasons why the doctrine called "the Trinity" is controversial is that this word is not found in the Bible. Yet, it is widely received in all kinds of Christian churches as the truth revealed in the Holy Scriptures for all believers to joyfully embrace and confess. The word is not found in the Bible, but the substance of the word is taught throughout the New Testament. Coming to rest easy with the idea that the One True God is the Three in One of the Trinity is better learned through the study of the way the Bible explains Who God Is. Rather than giving us a treatise on this subject, the Bible leads us to see this teaching by a process of introducing us first to God our Father. We are given a treatise on the subject of the resurrection in the Apostle Paul's first letter to the Christians in First Century Corinth. We are given much to ponder pertaining to the subject of Bible prophecy in the Olivet Discourse (recorded in Matthew 24, Mark 13, and Luke 21). By contrast, we are taught the Triune Nature of the One True God by an unfolding of His actions and will and traits, as the supernatural intervenes in the realm of the natural.

One of the most important Bible verses for me, personally, in the quest to get a handle on the subject of the Trinity of the One True God is what our Lord Jesus commanded His disciples to do, shortly before His ascension to the right hand of God the Father. Jesus told them (as we read in Matthew 28:19 and 20) to teach all nations, baptizing them in the "name of the Father, and of the Son, and of the Holy Spirit." This is very significant, even though it is only one unique Bible verse! It is highly significant because it would not make sense for the Apostles to baptize the nations into the Father, Son, and Holy Spirit, if it had nothing to do with explaining Who God truly Is. To be baptized into this Name invokes the eternal Personhood of each Entity mentioned by Christ. I see this as affirmation of real Deity.

Many Christians have debated the subject of what the baptizer was or is supposed to speak when a person receives the Christian covenantal washing with water. After all, the record in the Book of the Acts of the Apostles shows that those who believed the Good News were baptized "in the Name of the Lord Jesus." Why were they baptized in the Name of the Lord Jesus, when the Lord Jesus Himself told them to baptize "in the Name of the Father, and of the Son, and of the Holy Spirit"? Ellicott's Commentary provides some persuasive explanation of this apparent difficulty. The first years of the preaching of the Good News were limited to Jewish persons. These converts already knew the Father, and were familiar, due to Christ's teachings, with the Holy Spirit. But, the "nations" or Gentiles, who were to soon receive the Good News of the common salvation in Jesus Christ, were starting from the beginning, from scratch. This explanation makes a great deal of sense to me. Either way, since the fullness of the Godhead lives bodily in Jesus Christ, the words spoken by the baptizer would fulfill the command, either way.

There are many other passages that should be cited, if a Christian seeks to do a serious study of the subject of the Trinity. Sufficient for me, in my goal of seeking to be assured in my own heart and mind that this teaching is truly from our Lord and His holy Apostles of the First Century, is that it's truthfulness seems to be absolutely irrefutable, if we see the Bible affirming that Jesus Christ came as God with us, and that He is plainly declared to be God in the Bible. Hebrews opens by making it clear that Jesus is much more than a Messianic prophet or priest, but is, in fact, God. He is declared by God the Father to be God in the opening chapter of the letter that we commonly call "The Book of Hebrews".

As to how we should teach the doctrine of the Trinity, I am of the opinion that we do well to present the relationships as the Bible does. The Bible most frequently refers to God when speaking of the Father, so we should, too. It is through our Lord Jesus Christ, and by the workings of the Holy Spirit, that we are able to come to know the Father. We do well to be as close to the Bible in method as we can.

WHY IT'S HARD TO CHANGE

The human being is probably designed by the Creator to crave social stability. Much of what troubles us about our environment is the jolting experiences when our norms are interrupted by things that are commonly regarded as negative. A worker finds out that his or her job is gone, due to departmental cutbacks or downsizing. We find out that somebody we care about who very recently seemed to be the picture of health is diagnosed with a life-threatening condition. Closer to home, for some, a husband or wife announces that the marriage isn't working for them, and it wasn't something the other person saw coming. These are jolting things, and a thousand other everyday examples could be cited! We put these kinds of things on the list of what can set back the optimistic attitudes of persons generally very positive.

Change of thinking is just as traumatic, when it forces us to re-think things that trusted teachers in church life reinforced. Part of a happy Christian childhood is learning Bible stories and the best kinds of lessons from people who we are blessed to know in the household of the communion of Christians. We know that we are fallible, and that only God is incapable of error. But, for most of us who set out to live for God, we trust the ordinary convictions that we share with the people who invested time to help us come to know the Bible. Unless there is a good reason to challenge what we learned in our churches, we are not usually the kind of people who go around fixing things that do not happen to be broken.

But, IF you are raised to believe that the Bible is the Word of God in such a way that it trumps all other sources of good and positive authority, you are potentially in a dilemma. What if it becomes a fact that what you are reading from the Bible is undeniably different from what your favorite religious instructors are saying? What if you are convinced with all of your heart that Jesus is Lord, and that the Bible actually should be read without deception or twisting its words, to the best of our ability? Most of the time, it is a matter of interpretation. Brothers and sisters in one kind of church are taught to see this passage or chapter or book one way, and fellow Christians from other backgrounds are taught differently. In these cases, you can weigh the arguments from both sides, but you are not standing alone with a small minority on that issue. For example, some Christians emphasize the importance of receiving baptism and teach it as a condition of receiving forgiveness of sins. Others teach that baptism has nothing to do with actually causing forgiveness. There are many millions on both sides of that issue!

But, what if something comes up where there are Bible passages that make not only your fellow worshippers nervous in the local church you attend, but the pastor as well? What if you are given excellent reasons to feel that you should not even talk about that part of the Bible? What if this is happening in a church where we make a humongous deal about how much we respect the inerrancy of the God-breathed Holy Scriptures? Should you simply ignore the matter? Are you sinning if it bugs you that the people of God have become just as politically correct about a Bible verse as the unbelievers on college campuses who need so-called "safe places" to run and hide from hearing anything that fails to please them? Aren't we who claim to believe that the Bible is true the biggest hypocrites when this happens in our churches? Just thinking out loud. God help us do better for His glory.

Change really, really, really is a major trauma for many people in church life, and we've all seen it. There are persons who felt anxiety when a visitor sat in the pew that they normally used, and which all of the regular attenders knew to be occupied by that person. Add to that being called upon by the Lord Jesus to rethink something that you have regarded as too settled for too long to be questioned by anybody? Can that happen? When large numbers of Christian have been mistaken on a matter, the change is never painless. The world is round and not flat. Christians could do fine up into the 15th Century without knowing this scientific truth. Eventually, it was important for Christians to accept it! So it goes!

POVERTY AND THE BIBLICAL LAST DAYS

Is there any relationship at all between a Christian's view of the Biblical last days and the Christian desire to eradicate poverty from the face of the earth? The question is not, "do we know how to eradicate poverty at this point in history?" The question is not, "are Christians who defend economic liberty and low taxes bad or good?" The question is not, "are Christians who want governments to tax the wealthy more to eradicate poverty bad or good?" The question is as simple as it sounds, which is, "Can we logically consider the possibility that our view of the Biblical last days can influence the effort to make poverty into a non-existence fact of human history?" If there is a connection, then Christians who are preaching that we should love God and leave the last days far behind us are not merely attempting to win some kind of inter-Christian philosophical debate. We are not merely trying to say "aha, our side is right, and your side is wrong." We are thinking about something as practical as Dr. Salk curing polio, or the British Lord Witherspoon working to end the evil trade of human slavery. And, it doesn't really matter which political party, if any, ends up getting the most credit, if our question is answered. If it is possible that viewing the Biblical last days as entirely fulfilled in the First Century can help us find ways that our practical and reliable to end poverty, then we ought to be willing to consider this possibility.

First of all, having proposed such a dramatic possibility, let me admit that I am not there yet. I cannot prove that we can, in fact, find a "cure" for poverty, if every Christian comes to agree with me that there is a connection between the end of the last days as history and the idea that the kingdom of God is totally transforming our world through Christians in each new generation of mankind. I would not raise the issue, if I did not suspect that the possibility is there, however. I believe that the possibility is there that we can eradicate cancers of every type someday, so why not poverty? But, someone might ask, "what in the world does the problem of poverty have to do with the beliefs common among Christ's disciples about last days?" That is a fair retort, and I'll make an earnest effort to make my case that it is possible that we can end poverty someday, and that part of the energy is related to the Christian vision of the Biblical last days. It is not the only ingredient of high social progress goals, but it is one factor.

One of the realities of life which all of us see on the news frequently is war. When we do, whether or not we realize it, we who are Christians file away in our minds some amount of determination as to what it probably means about the times we live in. If we conclude that it means that we are currently "living in the last days" of human history, what accompanies that conclusion? Is it not a resignation to the notion that very little of the human condition, beyond the spiritual preparation for eternity, can be effected by how we live? We can hardly believe that we are living in the final days of the course of civilization, as we know it, and feel compelled to tackle a problem as difficult and challenging as the root causes of poverty. Why even study the root causes of poverty if we can do little or nothing to change it? What happens if the devout follower of God through Christ is thereby disinterested in the study of ways to eradicate poverty? The vacuum is left to dreamers who have only a materialistic vision of life. This leads to some cold-hearted solutions to the problem of poverty, such as forced abortions of as many vulnerable potential humans as possible, in many cases. It also compels many social planners to look to euthanasia as the means to make certain that humans die before the years that are defined as "non-productive".

What is the alternative to ways of ending poverty that upholds the dignity of the human as the highest order in the creation? It is for committed Christians to explore the root causes of poverty within the societies of mankind, and to study the things which answer the need for stability and security without violating human rights. To invest intellectual energy and scientific effort, and real dedication to actually finding reliable longterm solutions that make sense and fit with human liberty, the only motivation that can likely make this happen is the belief that God created our world to last and not be destroyed.

THE MEETING IN THE AIR

For me, reading what the Holy Spirit inspired the Apostle Paul to write to the Christians living in First Century Thessalonica was a major hurdle! Why is this? Because it seems to be telling the readers that all of the Christian believers in the whole world would be physically gathered to meet the Lord Jesus Christ. If this is the destiny of all Christians in our future, or else, if it was the destiny of all Christians living in the First Century, it is hard to explain. For most of the centuries of the outworking of the kingdom of God, it has been the case that very few have gone on record with a very complete explanation of these passages. (See First Thessalonians 4: 13-17). Some folks laugh at any Christian that takes these verses seriously. Some people have built their Christian experience around these verses. Does the admonition to love God and leave the last days behind help us come to a Biblical attitude that is also sensible?

First of all, the physical removal of all of the living Christians from Planet Earth would appear to contradict what Jesus Himself prayed for His followers, as recorded in the 17th Chapter of the Gospel of John. In verse fifteen of this high priestly prayer of Jesus, our Lord specifically asks the Father NOT to take His disciples out of this world. If, in fact, the plan of God was the removal of Christians from the world, whether in the First Century or many centuries later, this would seem to be a situation hard to understand nor explain very well. But, if our Lord was actually asking that His disciples NOT be removed from the world, and if that prayer was answered, then the proper and correct interpretation of the language of meeting Christ in the air has to be something other than a "rapture" of all Christians into heaven.

What are the Christian believer's options, who loves the Bible, and desires to be faithful to all of its glorious truths, including difficult passages to interpret? One option is to see how these words to the believers in Thessalonica fit with the Gospels. Maybe there is a match. It's worth looking into! In fact, the language of this letter can be viewed as fitting well with the Gospels! Three Gospel chapters, one from Matthew, one from Mark, and one from Luke, all agree that Jesus foretold the ruin and end of the Jewish Temple Age, which occurred in 70 A.D. In these three Bible chapters, Jesus spoke of His coming to gather His followers, said it would occur within that generation, and used language that matches quite well with the words that the Holy Spirit spoke to the First Century Thessalonians through Paul. Something major, of eternal importance, was about to take place, and did take place. Was it the physical removal of the living Christians from the earth? Or, was it the impartation of their guaranteed reward of immortality? Could these words have had a spiritual fulfillment?

The persecuted Christians of the First Century were called the "firstfruits of the Gospel" and they had a special reward coming for living through that initial period of transition out of the Old Covenant and into the New Covenant. Jesus told them in Matthew 16:28, "Some of you **STANDING HERE** shall not taste death until you see the Son of Man coming in His kingdom". He promised in the preceding verse to reward them at that time. This same promise of the soon-coming Son of Man is given to His people in the last chapter of the Book of Revelation, and verse 12. A special reward was granted to those who went through the First Century agony of being hated by their countrymen and Rome at the same time!

This analysis does not satisfy the craving for a "Left Behind Series" novel that's much more fun and sexy. But, it has helped me overcome what was a difficult obstacle in my personal journey to love God and leave the last days behind. The meeting in the air took place, and it united heaven and earth, as the Son of Man gathered His disciples into the permanent New Israel to transform the world! I cannot say that I understand these passages perfectly, but I do believe that the fact that Jesus prayed for God to keep His church in this world, and that the First Century believers were the target of this encouragement, and that it fits with words Jesus spoke concerning the destruction of Jerusalem, means it is fulfilled!

THE LAST DAYS AND AGNOSTICS

The end of the Biblical last days in the First Century is especially helpful to Christians who have occasional conversations about God and life with relatives or friends who are agnostics. Some agnostics and some atheists have studied the Bible and are aware that Jesus promised to come in His kingdom within the generation of people who were listening to Him teach during the First Century. They have wondered why more Christians are not concerned about the apparent failure of Jesus to know much about His coming. They have used this issue to reinforce their perception that we Christians are following a Prophet Who made a big mistake. We ought to be prepared to give a solid answer!

Jesus made no mistakes at all! Christians know this. Yet, some of the answers to the arguments of agnostics about Christ's guarantee to come in His kingdom to reward His saints and punish His enemies during the natural lifetimes of people living in the First Century seem to be too much of a stretch. Whenever any of us are caught in a situation where we cannot easily explain our way out of a difficult spot, there is always the temptation to try to help God out with methods that come short for both the integrity of the Bible and the sense of an objective standard. We can do better than that, and give our agnostic friends an answer that is sincere, compatible with reason, and directly in line with the words spoken by Jesus and the Apostles. But, it requires that we are willing to be persuaded that the popular teachings about end times could be in error! That's a huge thing for most Christians living in the 21st Century to consider, but many people could be helped when we do. There is a solid answer!

Many, many, many Christians have said that Jesus must not have meant to communicate that He would come back in the First

35

Century, because He obviously did not come. By saying that, these folks have been misled. We are misled on this issue for some reasons that can be cured. The Apostle Paul told the Christians living in First Century Corinth that they should arrive at truth about Scripture by comparing "spiritual with spiritual". But, what does that mean? Could it suggest that we can come closer to getting the Scriptures right if we line up the way God uses similar language expressions in His word? If so, then we might be able to see that what our natural minds demand in the implications of the word "coming" are completely in contradiction of what the Word of God teaches. One is right and one is wrong.

Babylon was destroyed in 689 B.C. Isaiah prophesied this destruction years before it came to pass. In the 13th Chapter of the Book of Isaiah, the war that utterly ruined forever the ancient City of Babylon is described in prophetic or apocalyptic language. Isaiah says that the Lord is "mustering an army", that they are being gathered "from the four winds" and "see the Lord is coming". He speaks of the sun, moon and stars ceasing to function for Babylon. In other words, God is going to put their lights out. God did not literally cause the sun, moon and stars to cease to function. These are terms descriptive of the war that brought God's judgment upon ancient Babylon. They are true, even though they are not given for the reader to understand in literal terms of the sun, moon, and stars falling or ceasing to function.

Jesus used the very same language to teach about the fall of First Century Jerusalem, including reference to the sun, moon, and stars. This was His "coming", just as the wrath of God was the day of the Lord, and His "coming" upon ancient Babylon, as Isaiah foretold it. So, when our natural minds demand a panoramic vision of Jesus Christ visually descending in modern times, we are demanding something that is contrary to what was the comparison of spiritual language of Isaiah with the spiritual language of the Lord Jesus. Some agnostics might even be able to respect such a response. Others won't, of course, but why not have a response that answers faithfully, logically, and in keeping with Biblical patterns?

THE LAST DAYS
AND CHURCH UNITY

Pastors tend to be very sensitive about harmony in the local assembly of Christians where they believe that the Holy Spirit has placed them, in order to help the family of believers to grow in the grace and knowledge of the Lord Jesus. The high calling of being a servant to Christians who regularly gather to worship God, build friendships, reach out to the community and the world, and nurture new generations of persons in the New Covenant blessings rightfully compels a pastor to resist any influence of change that seems to upset the unity of the local congregation. This is very understandable, just as it is in our family units. We cannot be healthy if we are constantly disputing things that we have accepted as settled.

However, the call to Christian unity is not rightfully intended by the Holy Spirit to be merely a way to end all disagreements about the meaning of Bible passages. Church unity is abused when the smug claims of "orthodoxy" amount to excuses to marginalize any Christian who draws attention to the Bible in a way that simply is not comfortable. We ought to be desirous, as the people of God in Christ, to examine Biblical truth claims in the manner of the Bereans. They were not the standard type of folks who ignore the foundations of truth claims, and strive simply for a popular groupthink. Instead, these believers living in First Century Berea were praised by the Apostle Paul for weighing carefully what they heard!

Today, it is reported that there are divisions in some congregations because of Christians who come to believe that the Biblical last days ended in the First Century. Any Christian who is a fair person, and who also loves the unity of the Spirit in the bond of peace, should hope for a non-emotional way of finding out who is causing this so-called "division". The immediate urge is to blame persons who hold to the minority persuasion on an issue like this. If they would just keep their mouths shut, then the division would not exist. That is a mistaken attitude, even a fleshly attitude, that does not glorify God at all! The root of the controversy must be examined in a manner that decent people see as just in courts of civil and criminal law. We expect certain standards beyond political correctness in our law courts.

A pastor in one of the Presbyterian denominations was threatened with disciplinary action because he taught that the Biblical last days ended in the First Century. The denomination is an evangelical one that tells the world that they believe the Bible to be inspired by God and inerrant. They affirm that the Bible is the foundation for teaching in the church, and also affirm what Reformed Christians call "sola scriptura". This particular pastor was not provided with an opportunity to explain from the Scriptures why he saw this teaching as correct. Because it appeared to be in conflict with the Westminster Confession, to those judging him, it did not seem to matter whether they could either prove or disprove his convictions from the Bible, even though they profess to believe in "sola scriptura". Even though they felt a certain appreciation for the idea that the Bible is sufficient to define our Faith, they would not consider the possibility that the great Westminster Confession was mistaken on this point. So, a form of political correctness and formalized Christian groupthink seems to sometimes overrule Biblical conviction.

Could it be that some group of responsible church leaders, well versed in the Bible, could have proven that this brother was mistaken about the fulfillment of the last days in the First Century? We'll never know, because such a principled and public approach to solving this matter was never permitted! And, so it goes in so many accounts of Christians and their leaders rejecting what the Bible says about the last days. This should be a major red flag to any Christian anywhere who deeply respects the principle of "sola scriptura". Yes, it's always possible that an individual who sees things from being only in the minority could be mistaken. But, when there is no honest, open, and public form of civilized examination allowed, you should beware! It is shameful for pastors to abuse church unity to silence Bible truth!

THE LAST DAYS AND OUR GENERATION

Some Christians might want to ask, "So, Paul, if the prophetic events are all behind us, what about us living right now? What about our generation? What is the Biblical attitude supposed to be about what is going on in the church and in our families and in the world?" In other words, what compels the connection of the people who lived out the Biblical last days in the First Century, and the rest of us? These are questions that come up for many Christians who try to think through the possibility that the last days are history. Every great movement needs a general game plan, and a set of common principles, and a sense of common expectations. For many Christians, the expectations of the hope of the Christian are somehow gone unless we are supposed to expect that the world and history will come to a close.

The kingdom of God operates from within all who love God through Jesus Christ, both in matters related to the life of the church, and to matters related to all that it means to be living in and working toward the goals that involve us in this world. The kingdom of God in its coming in during the events of the First Century changes some things for the Christian living today, but not everything. We are sons and daughters of the kingdom of God, and we are sons and daughters of Father Abraham, if we believe in the Lord Jesus Christ from the heart. So, we have been born into the world to live out our Christian calling in all of its aspects. The church of God in Christ has an ongoing kingdom mission, even though a major phase of that mission was completed in the First Century. It should not lead us to question why we are here when we come to see the last days as history. Yet, this happens for some Christians.

First, consider what is changed. There is no Battle of Armageddon foreordained. There is no great tribulation foreordained for us, nor any future generation of Christ's people! These are in the past. There is no reason to suspect that the world is getting worse and worse, because that was the expectation for the first generation of Christians awaiting the end of the last days of the Old Covenant. There is no reason to suspect that a worldwide dictator will arise who will force every person on the planet to accept the number 666 on his or her forehead. These are past fulfilled, if we are correct that the last days of the Bible really have taken place, as a normal reading of many passages demand. Another thing that all Christians should consider as applying only to the first generation of the Christian Faith in this world is the Apostle Paul's instruction that seemed to encourage being single over being united in the covenant of marriage. He said that his advice (never a command) to choose the single life over marriage was an accommodation to what he called "the present distress". After the Biblical last days ended and the fullness of the spiritual kingdom of God as His Isreal for all generations, the Church, fully replaced the Old Testament expression of God's Israel as the physical nation, based upon factors that included ethnicity, then it is true that there is no sense in which one should see the "signs of the times" as a factor regarding a marriage decision.

Secondly, let's think about what is unchanged for the Church. We still gather to give true and reverent worship to the Father through the Son in the power and presence of the Holy Spirit, with grateful hearts. We still celebrate the entrance into the kingdom of God by baptizing those who convert to Christ. Many Christians also celebrate the kingdom of God by baptizing little people who are born to practicing Christian households. We still enjoy the breaking of the Bread and the Cup, but only with a new and more special Presence Reality than the first generation of Christ's people did during the last days. They were remembering the death of their absent Lord, while Jesus Himself celebrates communion with us now! We still celebrate marriages contracted when both the husband and wife deeply love God and plan to form a Christian marriage for the glory of God. Beyond the church, the Christian today is freed from the bloody aspects of last days Bible prophecy, yet fully equipped with all of the positive promises of God!

THE LAST DAYS AND UTOPIAN EXPECTATIONS

The last two chapters of the Book of Revelation are beautiful descriptions of the New Heaven and the New Earth, as the restoration of the Garden of Eden. Included in this wonderful picture is the tree of life whose leaves are for the healing of the nations. This is a very interesting part of the prophetic drama! This is fascinating because we have been raised to believe that the New Heavens and New Earth are so radically different from the world as we know it. We learn of it in terms that seem to be utopian. This is not surprising because the language is very utopian. We are told that God will wipe away every tear, and that there will be no more death. These expressions have led many of us to think in terms of a society that is so removed from the world as we know it that it just cannot be the Christian church coming down from heaven to start the process of transforming the world into the glorious kingdom of God.

There are several things that compel me to think differently now than I use to about the New Heavens and the New Earth. For one, the death of death is a wonderful picture of what Jesus Christ has already accomplished for all who are His! He taught that no person who believes in Him will ever die, even if they physically die! This has to mean that physical death has never been the great enemy of the human soul. Rather, it has been the death that Adam and Eve died when they listened to the serpent and ate the forbidden fruit. That death has been totally reversed for all who enter the kingdom of God. Death has no lasting effect, because THE death has died! Physical death is only a steppingstone, so to speak, to the everlasting enjoyment of what we can begin to taste now, in the life of serving Jesus Christ.

The nations would need no "healing" if there was a sudden end to civilization as we have been taught in our traditional thinking about the New Heaven and the New Earth. The Church (that is, the Mother of us all spoken of by Paul in the Book of Galatians) hovers and yet, is among the people of God in Christ throughout the world. She is the Wife of the Lamb. She is the Church since the remnant of the Jewish nation were united with the redeemed First Century Gentiles into the One New Man, the Church, the Israel of God. So, Israel has truly been transformed out of the Old Testament expression into her eternal New Covenant expression as the ongoing and everlasting Gospel kingdom of God and His Christ!

The nations bringing their glory into the New Heavens and New Earth puts the beauty of the work God has done in perspective. Rather than an entirely other-worldly picture of a place where nothing about the world as we know it is happening, this is a place where much is happening. It is a busy world. The difference between the City of God and the world at large is that nothing impure enters the City. So, how can this be anything we have experienced yet? Our world is not that perfect! One television preacher has said, "If our world as we know it is the kingdom of God, I am disappointed!". Many Christians share that sentiment. But, should they? Are the utopian aspects of the New Heaven and the New Earth given to the reader for them to ponder a different natural environment.

Maybe, the New Heaven and the New Earth is given to contrast it with the Old Heaven and Old Earth that was given to man in the first creation. What was the main thing that Adam and Even enjoyed prior to the fall into sin? Fellowship with God was a regular special aspect of their lives. Christianity has brought about for many millions of people the delight of God living in His people, fellowshipping with His people, gathering His people to know Him and enjoy Him, and this is huge! Just think of what the world would be like if 99% of her inhabitants were living in daily communion with God through Christ, and learning His ways? The end of the last days in the First Century was followed by the descent of the fullness of the kingdom of God which is healing the nations. Millions have already entered.

THE LAST DAYS
AND CHRISTIAN ISSUES

Every Christian who is persuaded, as I am, that the war between the First Century Romans and the inhabitants of First Century Jerusalem brought about the time of the end of the Old Covenant has some parts of our outlook in common. Obviously, once you have become thoroughly convinced that Biblical last days ended in 70 A.D., then you do not have any reason to think that there are any more last days. Also, many references in the New Testament that refer to the day of the Lord or Christ coming soon or the coming of the Son of Man has a final fulfillment. Yet, it would be far from accurate to suppose that coming into the belief that the kingdom of God fully entered mankind in the events of the Jewish and Roman War necessarily causes Christians to agree about many other significant issues. For example, how has my current view impacted my thoughts about the creation narrative? What about the extent of the atonement? What about the differences Christians have regarding predestination? What about the best way to relate to our Jewish, Arab, Hindu, Buddhist, Agnostic, and all other neighbors? These are all matters where the Christian who desires to be prepared to give a solid answer for what he or she believes will still need to study ways to be a consistent Christian witness. Believing in the last days as behind us is a major help, in my opinion, but it is not by any means a panacea to answer all things.

So, it is important to attempt to explain ways in which this vital conviction has blessed my own thinking, at least, as I see it, in regard to major subjects that many Christians have found themselves in need of a good and sincere response. Those of us who have been privileged in life to have conversations with persons of a wide range of non-Christian backgrounds have been in different situations.

So, there is probably no "correct formula", for any Christian of any background to relate to non-Christians, beyond some general principles. One thing in common for all Christians is the desire to give a respectful and responsible answer to those who really want to know why we believe what we believe.

In this regard, there are some areas where I tend to believe that I am speaking for large numbers of Christians, and others where I am only representing my personal convictions. That distinction should be made whenever a person asks about a subject that compels a Christian response. For example, if a person wants to know what the majority of Christians at a given time in history believe about abortion, or evolution, or socialism, or anything else, I might not be able to provide a satisfactory answer. Yet, if I am asked, "Paul, why are you and other Christians so sure that Jesus rose from the dead?", I think I can offer something that sincerely reflects more than my own personal opinion.

So, how does the past complete fulfillment of the last days foretold in Holy Scripture differ from less than complete fulfillment, in how it informs or assists our ability as Christians to respond to various issues of great significance? I think it can be demonstrated that it helps us in some of these issues, and that it is not really a factor for our common Christian witness in regard to others. I'll try to address specific matters that fall into both categories. For example, in defense of the canon of the Bible as the complete and final written revelation from heaven, with no more expectation of God speaking in the authoritative manner that He did through the Apostles of the First Century, there is enormous help for Christians who accept the apostolic age as the end of the Biblical last days.

Christians have support, indirectly, from the fulfillment of Christ's words that the City of First Century Jerusalem would be destroyed for some Christian issues. While there is not a direct connection, for example, to our defense of Christ's resurrection from the dead, the fact that He accurately foretold a major war about forty years before it happened seems to be morally equal for all of us living since the First Century to the eyewitnesses of His miracles and those of His Apostles directly in the last days.

✝

THE LAST DAYS AND POLITICS

It seems to me that so many factors effect why anyone chooses to support a political party, so that it is not likely that believing in a particular interpretation of the Bible will necessarily lead to a partisan preference. While there are reasons for supporting some candidates over others, based upon their party's attitude toward Christians in general, I am not certain that it is effected greatly by any person's opinion concerning the last days. But, there are some things that probably are political attitudes which might follow from accepting that the Biblical last days were completed in the events of the First Century. They would not necessarily be partisan, but they would be significant things to consider.

My personal convictions in regard to how I think about politics is limited to the fact that I am an American, a Navy veteran, and that I grew up interested in seeing the government more conformed to what I perceive as a more constitutional set of limits on the government. Having said that, I am very well aware of the fact that there are millions of Christians who grew up seeing constitutional limitations on the actions of government as impediments to the advancement of civil liberties and civil rights. These fixed set of starting points in reasoning about the movements that shape the nation are only partly derived from direct Biblical teaching. This makes it difficult to spell out what a Biblical society ought to look like in a manner that almost all Christians can agree to, beyond the abundance of mercy, liberty, and equal opportunity as goals that seem to be compatible with loving God and loving our neighbor.

When we think about the desire to have a Christian attitude within politics that glories God concerning the global vision of what is right, then it might be true that we have some "hot spots" that are directly related to the most widespread vision of the Biblical last days. This would be the Christian desire to be a faithful representative of the kingdom of God in relationships both to our Jewish and Arab neighbors. The end of the Old Covenant system with the 70 A.D. fall of First Century Jerusalem has implications for the modern school of thought known as "Zionism". This influence is controversial, but is something which has grown into a movement over the last several centuries, and impacts our modern world.

So, it seems that believing that the Biblical last days ended in the First Century should lead to the conclusion that Christians achieve some things that appear to be conflicting, at first glance. We must be peacemakers, yet respect the principles of friendship, so as to be able to renounce the religious basis of Zionism at the same time as affirming that our modern Israeli neighbors have the right to live in peace. The modern Christian thinker who wants to take a stand for what is right has some hurdles, in my view.

It appears that church organizations which have moved to the very far left of center in regard to their rejection of the Scriptures as inspired by God, and their opposition to how the Bible defines marriage, and in regard to whether an unborn child should ever be thought of as possessing the right to be alive, these groups have been willing to only align themselves with the Palestinians. At the same time, it appears to me that church organizations that radically deny that any part of the last days was completed in the First Century are so pro-Israel that they have no sympathy at all for the Palestinians! In the middle are many Christians who love both Jews and Arabs. This is where I anticipate that more of Christ's followers will find themselves if God brings about the widespread acceptance of the normal reading of many New Testament passages which teach us that the Biblical last days took place in history. On many other political subjects, it is only a guess as to how most Christians will translate their views of the Bible into the kinds of political activities and movements that they feel led to support.

THE LAST DAYS ACCORDING TO KARL MARX

Many defenders of the system of governing society known as "communism" have resented the notion that Karl Marx was essentially a religious prophet of the last days, without the assumptions that favor religion. In other words, his views were expressed in highly charged terms related to his views about wealth accumulation, labor, what he perceived as the evils of capitalism, and how mankind would overcome its struggle against these "evils". His "dialectic" was assessed by its critics as taking the same models of the orthodox Christian teachings about creation, the fall of man from the Garden of Eden, recovery through Christ, and reversing the main characters, producing what amounts to a dogmatic interpretation of the whole unfolding of human history, only with materialistic causes and outcomes.

Marx envisioned a day when the so-called "oppressed" workers of the world would unite and throw off forever their tormentors, the owners of the means of production. Somehow, without any contradiction, all individualism would be replaced with united human ownership of all material possessions, and equal distribution of all material possessions, with each contributing labor, and nobody individually owning anything of material value. All private ownership would be eradicated in a new spirit of human brotherhood and without any further need for anyone to try to obtain more stuff than another.

The process in the meantime, was the "dialectic", which has to do with the struggle to end the evils of individualism and private ownership of wealth. This part of the process requires violence, as those who have obtained great wealth will not voluntarily surrender their good fortune. Among those who try to defend a less bold vision than the most dramatic teachings of Marx on this subject, they insist that his goal of achieving a form of materialistic egalitarianism without violent struggle is achievable by the democratic process of people learning to simply vote for high taxation on all who possess great wealth and the use of government programs to dispense more money and services to themselves.

Our world was most definitely influenced by those who proceeded Marx in their passionate belief in some sort of establishment of egalitarian society, and the advent of modern wars to enforce goals derived from the thinking of social engineers like Karl Marx. At minimum, this should indicate to all people that a basic familiarity with the study of the last days has a powerful impact upon human actions! To think that it is some sort of irrelevant footnote in the intellectual pursuits of nerds, and is disconnected to real world events such as war and peace, is to close our eyes to historic reality.

The Christian alternative to Karl Marx is not always popular, but offers thinking human beings so much more. The major schools of the study of the last days within the Christian Faith that have matured to a large degree in modern times have a range of positive and negative features, but none of these four or five Christian philosophies of human history and anticipations for the future of mankind eliminate private ownership, individualism as an important basic reflection of the Creator Himself, and none end up making it imperative that human beings must empower themselves by stealing what others have produced! My own view of the last days is the least popular among modern Christians right now, but it goes further than the competing Christian views, in that it eradicates all reason to believe that the violence associated with the events of the last days are somehow guaranteed by the Bible for people living since the First Century A.D. But, ALL Christian views of eschatology show respect for natural rights and liberties of human beings, whereas the view of Karl Marx and socialists utterly despise such beautiful gifts of the loving Creator. Thinking about history and the study of last days most definitely has real life consequenses, not only for ourselves, but for how stable or else rotten we make the future for our children and grandchildren. To love God and and leave the last days behind is to truly love our posterity!

✝

THE LAST DAYS
AND THE AFTERLIFE

Heaven and hell drive more than a few members of the human family to think about God. This fact has been used by critics of all organized religion to accuse Christianity of being a powerful drug for religious teachers to manipulate human guilt. While I reject the presumption that the majority of preachers, priests, and other leaders in any organized religion, most especially the Christian tradition, are motivated by human fear manipulation, I do think some have been, for sure! Also, I think that the thoughts of human beings about how to be reasonably certain of a positive experience vs. a horrifying experience after death is a legitimate source of serious pondering for all of us. Does the teaching that we ought to love God and leave the last days behind challenge the traditional Christian teaching after heaven and hell?

The short answer is "yes". If you accept the fact that the last days were begun in the First Century and ended when the City of Jerusalem was destroyed by the Romans in 70 A.D., and if you also believe that the events in the Book of the Revelation of Jesus Christ as Conquering King are to be understood in light of fulfilled prophecy from Jesus and the Apostles, then it will lead you to think differently about what we commonly call the "afterlife". It may or may not change your view of heaven and hell completely, but it will be certain to challenge some of the traditional Christian interpretations on this subject.

The reason why this is definite is that we are told in the Book of Revelation that "death and hades were thrown into the Lake of Fire". Obviously, a lake of fire is a figurative expression. Also, the particular

49

death that was thrown into the lake of fire is related to the evil spiritual realities of those persons who were also thrown into the lake of fire. If you conclude, as I have, that this happened in the Biblical last days, then it raises some questions related to what happens to human beings now when they die. Do they simply cease to exist? Do they face their Creator and Judge? Do they inherit eternal bliss? Do some of them experience the wrath of God? What is the nature and length of that experience of His wrath?

Some Christians accept the past fulfilled truth because it helps them think that they are rid of the notion of everlasting punishment. Some Christians deny the truth of past fulfillment because they think that it makes it too easy for people to get rid of the notion of everlasting punishment. Personally, I think that either attitude regarding the idea of everlasting punishment are less than wise and less than valid!

Death and Hades thrown into the Lake of Fire, even though words of symbolism and apocalyptic, have enormous implications for the fact that no person who dies in the Lord Jesus Christ has to wait any longer in any resting place for all of the joys of the reunion with loved ones and the fullness of the presence of God. There is no abode of the dead for those who have put on immortality through the gracious blessing of being in Christ! There is no wait. Yet, we do not know exactly what the exact experience is for anyone, whether the person in Christ who is guaranteed everlasting joy, nor the wicked, who are not guaranteed everlasting joy. Hebrews 9:27-30 states what seems like an ongoing norm for all human beings in all generations, when it tells us that every person is going to die, and after that, will come a personal judgment. So, we cannot be fully persuaded by the apocalyptic language in the Book of the Revelation about the nature of the wicked, or whether they are tossed into the Lake of Fire, because that very well could be limited to the judgment that happened in 70 A.D. But, we should not be arrogant, even if there is no proof that the wicked eternally are conscious of their rebellion, because we will all face the Judge. For believers, life will never end and biological death is a graduation! For those who deliberately reject God and His Christ, there is certainty from Scripture that He will hold a meeting with them. Because of what is past fulfilled, I don't know for certain that everlasting punishment means the same thing for those who die in rebellion now as it did for those who were punished in the 70 A.D. event. It could be the case! But, I am confident that all who call upon the Lord Jesus with true faith in His resurrection have everlasting life.

DON'T ABUSE THE WORD "ORTHODOX"

Every Christian's personal convictions about Bible prophecy is "orthodox".....if only a handful of Bible passages are important! The study of Bible prophecy issues, more than any other area where a person sets out to establish sound interpretation of the Holy Scriptures, involves being able to do more than simply grab a verse here and there. More than any other area of the study of the Bible, history is a part of the effort to rightly discern Bible prophecy. This is why it is all backwards for us in the modern era to think we can accurately get a handle on this subject by reading the tea leaves of the morning news! We go back to ancient history to find the future, if we want to be true to the methodology of reading Bible prophecy. We do NOT try to make guesses about what modern events seem to mean, or who might be the modern "anti-christ", etc. That is going about the process backwards, in regard to this holy Christian subject!

The truth of the matter is that there is no genuinely "orthodox" view of the subject of end times. In order to judge any deviation from the common Christian conviction, there has to be such a thing as a set of principles accepted very, very widely in many places, and demonstrated clearly from understandable exposition of the Bible. We Christians can do this in defense of the teaching that the One True God eternally exists in the Persons of the Father, Son and Holy Spirit, without ceasing to be the One and Only True God eternal. We can build a strong defense of justification by faith which always produces good works of obedience motivated by love. We can build a strong case for many other teachings directly from the Bible, so that when we express these convictions in confessions or creeds, they are not alien to any portion of the Scriptures, themselves. There is no Christian consensus about the subject of Bible prophecy, and there never has been, even among the church fathers! Christians who agree with Christ that He honored His promise to come back in the First Century are not heretics. Because it is a minority view, they are subject to the false charge. But, their accusers never rely upon the Bible to condemn them!

Look where "orthodoxy" has gotten the church, on the subject of Bible prophecy. There is absolutely no consensus about how to read the expression "a thousand years" in the 20th Chapter of the Book of the Unveiling of Christ as King over all. There is no universal consensus about whether the phrase "new heavens and new earth" should be understood as spiritual transformations in a covenant context, or the actual destruction and re-invention of the natural universe, as many Christians claim. Because these realities are essential to possessing close to a common framework for fitting the events revealed in the Scriptures together, cohesively, and with honor to the unity of the whole of the Biblical revelation, then we have much work to do before we can make a negative judgment about a brother's views on this matter. Yet, we do know that we agree, as evangelical Christians, that God has spoken to man authoritatively in His written revelation, and that He is able to truly enable us as His kids to come closer to agreement, if we place Him and His Word above our partisan Christian groupthink biases.

One of the proper starting points, which is neglected severely by most public preachers and teachers in all Christian groups, is a straightforward examination of the words recorded in the Gospels, and spoken by the Lord Jesus, that directly pertain to the Greek words translated as "coming". Any Christian who has a heart for truth should make a list of these word uses in the Gospels. That is a Christlike and Biblical start.

Since there is no genuine universal common Christian orthodox view of last things, this does not mean that there are no wonderful commonly respected principles. One principle of Bible study is to allow the most clear statements of Scripture to help all of us define the statements which are expressed in prophetic language. So, we are not there yet, when it comes to that possible Christian prophetic orthodoxy. We should desire to share a common interpretation that can reasonably free to explain from the Bible, just as our simple common Christian ability to relate to John 3:16.

SOME OF YOU STANDING HERE

Most modern American Christians deny that the coming of the Son of Man occurred in the timeframe that our Lord Jesus Christ said that it would. As shocking as this sounds, most Christians are agreeing with atheists on this issue, without realizing it, as well as others who oppose the Good News that Christ is Savior, Prophet, King and Judge. Those who are of a non-Christian religion, as well as agnostics or atheists, are not really behaving in any unusual manner by denying that Christ knew what He was talking about when He promised to come in the natural lifetime of some who were standing in His presence. But, it is a little weird that Christ's own disciples have a terrible time accepting His plain words!

The event that is commonly called "The Transfiguration" occurred within six days of our Lord speaking these words. (see Matthew 16: 27 and 28). This has compelled more than a few Bible readers, thinkers, and scholars to conclude that Jesus must have had this significant encounter in mind when He told His listeners, "For the Son of Man is going to come in his Father's glory with his angels, and then he will reward each person according to what he has done. Truly, I say to you, there are some standing here who will not taste death until you see the Son of Man coming in his kingdom." Was the Transfiguration the complete fulfillment of these words?

We read about the Transfiguration in Matthew 17. Jesus took Peter, James and John with him up on a high mountain. He was transfigured by becoming very bright. Elijah and Moses appeared. Peter offered to build three tabernacles. Then, the light went away, and they did not see Elijah and Moses. As they descended the mountain, Jesus told them not to talk about this until after His resurrection. In his second general epistle, the Apostle Peter referred to this event to demonstrate that he and the others were eyewitnesses of Christ" majesty in His power and coming. So, it was a powerful event, and perhaps it was a preview of the actual coming of the Son of Man.

Consider, however, the details that seem to be missing from the Transfiguration that Jesus said would take place when He would come in the glory of the Father. He said that angels would come with him. That did not occur during the Transfiguration. He said that every person would be rewarded for what he had done. This did not happen. The Apostles, themselves, had not yet begun their time of being commanded to go and teach all nations, let alone receive the reward for their service!

If the three Apostles who were eyewitnesses of the Lord's majesty was fulfillment of the coming of the Son of Man, then it proves more than what the futuristic bias might want to prove. We are told in very dogmatic fashion that this term has to mean an event related to the end of human history. If it could have meant the Transfiguration, then this proves that it does NOT require any still future interpretation.

The other alternative that is neither during the Transfiguration, nor at some indefinite end human history, is to make it mean the same thing that Jesus spoke of in Matthew 24, Mark 13, and Luke 21. He spoke of gathering the elect from the four winds at His coming, which was in the middle of His discussion about the fall of Jerusalem.

Some of you standing here most likely means that some of our Lord's First Century followers were still alive when the war began in 66 a.d. They recognized that this was what Jesus spoke about years before. They fled Jerusalem. What an amazing thing it would have been to see what their Lord spoke about decades earlier now beginning to unfold! They saw the coming of the Son of Man. They came through the most terrible persecution and now their reward was almost in hand! Thanks be to God.

CHRISTIAN FREEDOM TO
DISCUSS GREAT BIBLE THEMES

Family discussions range from fun subjects to details of our daily lives to great controversies about the major decisions we make in life. In some families, there is great freedom for a wide range of discussion without fear of severe alienation, and in others there is very little tolerance for much difference. This is part of what it means to belong to a household or a larger family clan. That same thing is true in spiritual terms among Christians. Some Christians are capable of a wide range of discussion, even when facing controversial issues, without being overwhelmed by stress and tension. Others, for whatever reasons, cannot handle very little discussion that is not tightly controlled. So it goes.

My own preference is toward a generous range of the freedom of Christians to discuss the Bible without somebody losing their lunch because the Bible subject is not their favorite topic. I think all churches and all pastors in all places should desire that kind of openness in the family of God. Again, that is my own preference. I am well aware that people can only be and do as their strengths and weaknesses, their advantages and limitations, permit them.

Some areas of the Bible are controversial because Christians are afraid that they will be disloyal to the church leaders who influenced them in the development of their walk with God if they dare to question any of the opinons taught by those leaders. Some areas of the Bible are controversial because two types of personalities absolutely cannot see the exact same verses of the Bible in the same way, for reasons that will only be explainable, I suppose, in the great beyond! But, some areas of the Bible are only in the category of "too hot to handle" because Christians have suppressed them. Just plain no likee-likee!

There are Christians for whom the very word "predestination", for example, makes them red in the face. They find themselves immediately aroused and prepared to go to war, with a passion to pronounce an anathema against any person who believes that predestination is true. Such are seen as the worst kind of scum-sucking slime that the world has ever known! It is a fortunate reality that the majority of anti-calvinists are not quite that demonstrative. Yet, it is very true that a great many people cannot tolerate a discussion of predestination. Some who love the subject, on the other hand, can hardly see how it shouldn't be the constant supply of all conversations! But, is it wrong to see the necessity of freedom to discuss the Bible passages that speak of predestination, and to have that conversation without emotion?

There are Christians who have decided in advance that they want nothing at all to do with the subject of Bible prophecy, especially, if there is going to be any discussion of the Bible passages that seem to teach a First Century fulfillment. The lack of Christian freedom to discuss great Bible themes has produced in church life what is not much different than the evil oppression of what we call "political correctness" in the social atmospheres in much of modern Western society. These are straitjackets in advance to prevent a discussion that could possibly result in thinking that makes some people uncomfortable. Instead, we need the freedom to communicate, which makes God comfortable, rather than just us.

SO ALL ISRAEL SHALL BE SAVED

The Apostle Paul began his treatise concerning ethnic Israel, as recorded in the 9th through 11th chapters of his letter to the Christians in First Century Rome, by expressing his willingness to be cut off from Christ, if this could cause his beloved nation to be saved! He knew this was impossible, but it expressed the intensity of his passion for his natural people who he greatly desired to be converted to their true Messiah Jesus Christ and be saved from the pending wrath that would their national and ethnic covenant. Soon, the events of history would unfold, and the Israel of God would include all who trusted Christ. Paul wanted as many of those persons to be ethnic Jews as possible. Paul was truly a Jew's Jew! It was an irony of destiny that he was the Apostle to the Gentiles, in spite of his strong national love.

Gentiles coming in to the covenant of God in Christ, the Christian Church, the Israel of God, needed to learn why they were being chosen to be ingrafted into Israel, while the majority of that generation of the last days of the nation Israel was losing out. God set apart an elect number, a remnant, from among all of the tribes of the Land of Judah and Israel, who were chosen to believe the Good News preached by the Apostles, receive baptism into the Faith, and to preserve Israel in her new and everlasting communion as the Christian Church among all nations. To fill up the host of "all Israel", God was calling many people from among the Gentiles through faith in Jesus Christ to become true spiritual Israelites, not according to circumcision nor ethnicity, but by confession that Jesus Christ is the One True Lord.

In Romans Chapter 11, verses 25 and 26, the drama of these three chapters seems to culminate. All Israel being saved is related to that first Christian generation living during the ministry of the Apostles.

This was the first generation of Christianity as the New Covenant expression of the kingdom of God and the final generation of ethnic Israel as God's covenant nation. The "fullness of the Gentiles" who came in during this first generation of Christianity were those who believed the Good News and were added to Israel. They called upon the Lord Jesus. Together, the remnant of ethnic Israel who were true spiritual Israelites, and the many Gentiles added to the Faith who were now spiritual Israelites, became the permanent Temple of the Holy Spirit forever and ever, replacing fully the physical temple.

Many Christians have not read these three chapters together to see them as a cohesive unit of instruction about the plan of God. This has resulted in expectations throughout the centuries, especially after the rise of the United States, built upon millennial hopes to discover the kingdom of God in a way unknown before, that somehow a distinction exists between Christ's Wife the Church, and the Israel of God. They are actually one and the same and they are neither uniquely Jewish nor Gentile. The Israel of God did, in fact, have many national, ethnic, political, and social distinctions for the centuries of her history from her beginning to the time of Christ. Yet, always, she was primarily a people called out by Yahweh to be in covenant with Him as a spiritual family, and not just a special gene pool.

Today, to be a true descendant of Abraham and Sarah is to believe in the Seed of Abraham, Who is Jesus Christ Who fulfilled all of the Old Covenant prophesies, and Who as the Hope of Israel reigns on the throne of King David over heaven and earth. In Him are all of the spiritual blessings that we can envision or hope for. Rather than a political kingdom on earth, Christ works from within His people to make His kingdom grow and grow and grow in each new generation of humanity, as true Israel enlarges.

LIVING WITHOUT THE EXPECTATION OF THE LAST DAYS UPON US

There are many millions of human beings in our world who believe that we are presently living in the Biblical last days. The dogma that mankind is now living in the last days is incorporated into several systems of interpreting the subject of Bible prophecy. Also, it is part of Islam. In one volume of work written about this subject, the view that we are not living in the last days is criticized as depriving the modern Christian of the basis for our Christian hope. But, is that true? Is our hope actually based upon the notion that various wars are going to occur, with people receiving the mark of the beast in order to carry on business, and that the world must end in a blood Armageddon? Is that truly the substance of the Christian hope? I think not. Christ Himself is the Substance of the joy of believers in good times and not so good times. Understanding the Biblical last days increases our hope, rather than lessening it!

It is sad to me that large numbers of my sisters and brothers have rejected the truth that the Biblical last days are behind us. I think that I understand some of the reasons why it is discomforting for some to think about the possibility that the Biblical last days ended in the First Century. For many, it is very uncomfortable because it makes them part of the minority in the church. For others, it is because they see the world as a place that can only be made into a decent reflection of the best and noblest values if it is just destroyed by the wrath of God and replaced with a whole new invention! Others are not sure where modern man fits into the plan of God for the ages, if the Biblical last days have ended.

You are open to being asked to explain why the majority of people disagree with you when you embrace the past fulfillment of the Biblical last days in First Century history. That is an impossible task! How can you know with absolute certainty what deep motivations keep people from affirming what you affirm? But, you are automatically granted less than a fair level of reasonable credibility, solely because you are in the Christian minority. This reminds me of the Senators questions then-Judge Clarence Thomas when he was being considered for the Supreme Court. Several were astounded that Professor Anita Hill would just make up the accusations against him that Judge Thomas vehemently denied. He was asked, "Why do you think she would say these things?" He responded with the honesty that characterized all of his responses. He said that he could not possibly know what was in the mind of another human being.

Why is it that only the minority of Christians have taken the position that the words of the Lord, as recorded in Matthew 24, Mark 13, and Luke 21 came to pass in the generation that He said it would take place in? We know some of the reasons, without needing to guess, because countless books have been written by authors who absolutely insist that Jesus did not intend for His words to be understood as about to be fulfilled in the First Century. Most have said some version of the idea that one has to realize that apocalyptic language can have more than one meaning. So, when Jesus said, "this generation shall not pass away until all of these things are fulfilled", that could mean something different from the idea that the reader should expect the things that Jesus foretold to occur within that particular generation. Why is that? It seems that they think that Jesus allowed Himself a flexible definition of generation.

Others say that two different questions were answered by Jesus. After Jesus told His disciples that the stones of the beautiful temple they were admiring would one day be thrown down and utterly destroyed, the disciples asked Him when this was going to happen. In Matthew's account, they asked Him also when He would come. In Mark's account and in Luke's account, there is no way to force their question into two separate questions. But, since they can do this with Matthew's account, they do. So, they wanted to know two things, as these folks understand Matthew's account: 1) when will it be that the temple in Jerusalem, along with the City of Jerusalem, be destroyed?; and 2) when will you come? According to this interpretation of Matthew's account, Jesus gave them a series of events that were going to unfold in a way that combined the two very distinct questions into one answer. The answer He gave required them to know how to separate the parts of His answer which applied to the destruction of Jerusalem and the temple from the parts of His answer that applied to the end of human history and human civilization. They claim that Jesus was speaking to both. Noteworthy is that there are no significant differences in the substance of Christ's answer found in any of the three accounts! Mark and Luke record the question as obviously related to the timing of the destruction of the City and temple, with absolutely no allusions at all to any event far in the future from that catastrophe! Yet, we are told to take Matthew as giving us what they really meant to ask, even if we have to stretch their words.

Why are most Christians afraid to consider the possibility that the events of Bible prophecy are history? Some say that it is impossible that the overwhelming majority of Christians for nearly 2000 years could possibly be mistaken about a matter as important as this. Now, we're getting to the heart of the issue before us. So, we have to ask, "Is it possible for the overwhelming majority of people to be wrong?" Is that doable? Have we seen that happen before? Is there precedent for suspecting that sometimes the majority can be dead wrong, even on an important issue?

It seems important to voice sympathy with the idea that the Christian Church cannot be totally wrong on a vital issue, because, at some point, it effects the confidence of the Christian in God's ability to protect and preserve His truths in all generations of mankind. If the church can be mistaken about the matter of the last days, doesn't this suggest that she cannot be the "pillar and ground of the truth" that the Apostle Paul stated that she is? In response to this, it is very true that the church is the pillar and ground of the truth, and she is the possessor of the great truths of the ages. She preserved the Holy Scriptures for our hope and blessing in dark times and we have them because of her. So, we have the whole truth that is necessary for our salvation and growth in grace, because the church kept her trust to keep the Scriptures, even when it meant great sacrifice. But, that is not the same thing as being infallible in her ability to interpret the Holy Scriptures. That claim of several bodies of professing Christianity is a view that has no warrant in the Scriptures themselves, nor in Jesus, nor in the Apostles. So, it's very possible for the majority of Christians to possess together the truth of a matter, without the majority of Christians being willing nor motivated to come to grips with that area of truth.

Some areas of Bible truth are simply very unpopular. Christians, like everyone else, are not thrilled about getting their heads chopped off. This is why more than a few of the unpopular teachings in the Bible are either ignored, denied outright, or else, suppressed. Not that many Christians show up for a theological party with coffee and predestination, for example. The same is true when a Biblical view of end times goes against the popular grain of the culture.

So, here's the facts. Christians who embrace the idea of the Biblical last days as history are giving up a few goodies. These include the Battle of Armageddon, the Great Tribulation, the endless search for the last days Man of Lawlessness nor the Antichrist, as these are all characters in a major dramatic showdown between the message of the Apostles and the rulers of the Old Covenant Nation of Israel. But, leaving the last days behind does not mean losing our permanent covenantal connection with all of the saints of all nations, languages and generations. The whole family of God in Christ from all ages, and generations, are the true Israel of God through Jesus Christ the Seed of Abraham, and are all together and forever united spiritually in the everlasting kingdom that Christ brought to man, whether we are in heaven or in earth.

GALLILEO AND THE LAST DAYS REFORMATION AND REVOLUTION

Why was Galileo declared pretty close to a heretic by the Pope and forced to live out his life in house arrest? He died at 77 years of age in 1642. The controversy that engulfed his life started a century sooner when Nicolaus Copernicus advocated the idea that the sun is the center of the solar system that we live in, and that the earth and other planetary bodies move around the sun. Galileo provided the research to prove the rightness of the claims of Copernicus. But, his work was denounced and was accused of being incompatible with both the principles of philosophy and theology. The argument among theologians, philosophers, and humanist thinkers had to do with the merits of either a "geocentric" or else a "heliocentric" solar system. Almost unanimously the church saw the claims of Copernicus and Galileo as contrary to the sense of Holy Scripture. So it seemed to church leaders in that century that the spread of the idea that earth rotates around the sun was designed to undermine the faith in the authority of the Bible, which many saw as teaching the absolute opposite.

Nearly four centuries since the passing away of Galileo and it does not appear that religion has been devastated by the common agreement among most believers and non-believers that the earth rotates around the sun. If Galileo and modern science got it right, the organized church at that time was suppressing him for reasons of their own misunderstanding of the Scriptures, and not any actual heresy. In other words, what Galileo sought to prove is not incompatible with Scripture properly discerned, prayerfully, and carefully, and thoughtfully, with minds that are governed by the fearless love of the truth, and not fearfulness. At any rate, the controversy proved that there was a way, while being faithful to the reverence due to Scripture, to understand the language that appeared to say that the earth does not move.

There are reasonable explanations for the fact that the opening chapter of the Book of Genesis appears to present the story of creation of God entirely from earth's point of view. One is that this was the best way our Creator could communicate His covenant. There are many people far more qualified than I am who post excellent discussions of this subject. What about serious Christians who want to be faithful to the actual meaning of Scripture and also think about, study, and enjoy science? What things are truly science and what claims are more accurately described as "atheist philosophy posing as science"? We want to oppose atheism posing as science WITHOUT ever inhibiting bold pursuit of all that man can learn about how our marvelous created order works. So, this is not really an essay about how to enjoy science while maintaining a consistent Christian philosophy of science. Rather, it is the connection between hyper-popular religious errors and the fact that such mistakes tend to discourage scientific curiosity.

In a bit of irony, the church was opposing Galileo's research because it was thought that his conclusions represented an assault upon the literal method of Bible interpretation. In the case of Christians today who are socially ostracized for believing the plain words of Christ, the intense opposition of religionists to these Christians is because they are taking the Bible at face value. This is understood, I think, of being able to cause a last days reformation and revolution. Still, Galileo was perceived to be threatening the literal reading of Bible passages, whereas religionists today accuse those Christians who read the words of Jesus and the Apostles concerning the last days in literal language of being heretical, or close!

Truth wins eventually in church and in all other venues. Time has vindicated Copernicus and Galileo. The reverence for the Scriptures, and the development of Christian theology, adapted and incorporated the discovery of these two scientists quite well. This will be true of the day when it is no longer forbidden to tell the truth in church about what Jesus and the Apostles said about the Biblical last days. Just as it is important to place all truth above our comfort zones, so it's true we should leave that the Biblical last days behind us, because they were fulfilled, according to our Lord Jesus, in the 1st Century.

THE UNKNOWN DAY AND HOUR
THAT PROVES TOO MUCH

We have grown up as Christians so saturated with the dogma that Christ's Second Advent is still a physical, visible and future event to end history that it has forced otherwise straightforward Christian teachers to stretch to the limits the meanings of plain words. Theologians feel compelled to find a future event in Christ's discussion with His disciples about the destruction of the Temple. Matthew 24, Mark 13, and Luke 21 all record this discussion. In Mark and Luke, there is no loophole for inventing the future Second Advent. But, theologians, like those federal judges who can find anything that fits with their cultural or political outlook in the Constitution, (invisible to others, but they see it clearly!), so it is that the emotional need to support the dogma of a future physical Second Advent is so strong that they find it!

Matthew gives a slightly different account of the question raised by the disciples than does Mark and Luke. It is extremely difficult for me to see how they can be so absolutely certain that Matthew is recording two very radically different questions, when it is obvious that Mark and Luke record the disciples as asking only one essential question. Jesus told the disciples that the buildings of the Temple that they were admiring would one day be thrown down and utterly destroyed. In all three accounts, the disciples wanted to know when this would happen. In Matthew's account, one can (if they are predetermined to do so), find something beyond the event in the second part of the question, which was, "and what will be the sign of Your coming?" This is all of the proof that they need to insist that the subsequent verses are combining Christ's prophecy of

Jerusalem's doom with a far distant narrative of Him coming at the end of human history.

After describing His coming, Jesus told His disciples, "this generation shall not pass away until all of these things take place". In normal reading, that would not be regarded as controversial or out of touch with the story to understand Jesus to say that His coming, as described in this chapter, anyway, would take place within a generation. But, no, the defenders of religion cannot tolerate that possibility, as it does not fit with what they feel compelled to teach. They are aware that if they admit that these words mean pretty much what they appear to mean, that they are hard-pressed to prove from the Bible that Jesus plans to visually come to the planet and terminate human history. So, they will force arbitrary applications of passages away from the destruction of First Century Jerusalem, and to the end of time, as they see it.

One bonanza in this scheme is the fact that, after telling His disciples that all of the prophesied events would happen in that First Century generation in which they were living, Jesus told them, essentially, "no man knows the day nor the hour when the Son of Man is coming". Rather than reading this in its normal meaning in context, these interpreters say "aha, what further proof do we need that a future, physical and visible second coming of Jesus is part of the discussion?" The truth is, as they probably know very, very well, that it is quite possible to know that some things are going to take place within a specific generation, and yet, not know which day and hour when that major event is going to occur. You could set up a visit with a family member or friend for a certain weekend. It is possible that, due to not being able to be precise about this or that related to the visit, you could agree that someone will just show up anytime on a certain day. Perhaps, with the ability to indicate morning, afternoon, or evening. In an event that is most of a generation away, as of the teaching of Christ before His crucifixion, then the day nor the hour doesn't change that one bit. It is sad that the people of God are so thoroughly confused about this matter, and they know better than to ask their pastor, in too many situations.

THE UNKNOWN TIMES AND EPOCHS OF ACTS 1: 6 AND 7

One of the questions and answers in the Bible that has puzzled me has been found in the 6th and 7th verses of the Acts of the Apostles written by Dr. Luke. It is a fairly simple question posed to the Lord Jesus by His disciples just prior to His ascension. Jesus had told them to wait for the empowerment of the Holy Spirit Who would soon come to them. They asked Him if He would restore the kingdom to Israel at this time. Instead of giving them a straight "yes" or "no", Jesus told them it was not for them to know the times and the epochs which the Father has placed in His own hands. He redirected them to focus on their mission of being His witnesses and completing the assignment to teach and baptize all nations.

By the time of Christ's resurrection some features of how the end times would play out were already known. They knew that the Temple in Jerusalem would be destroyed within one generation. They knew that they were going to suffer for the Gospel message and the Name of their Savior, and that some of them would even have to die for the Faith. But, they did not know about the relationship between the unfolding of the kingdom of God and their beloved ethnic nation. What would become of the Jewish nation? When would the Old Testament prophecies come to pass that foretold a great time of Jewish dominance in the world? When would it be that all nations would flow to Jerusalem? The answer that they were given by Jesus was one which left them still not knowing for sure if or when their nation would be restored to its prophesied glory among all nations of mankind. Instead, it was not for them to know.

History has unfolded quite differently than Jewish people of the First Century anticipated. Not only has it not been the case that the physical Throne of David has been set up in Jerusalem, but their chief City of First Century Jerusalem was ended along with their Temple, as the prophecy of the Lord Jesus Christ came to pass. The Temple has never been rebuilt. So, either the Old Testament prophets were not speaking in hyper-literal terms for the Israelites, or else, as the more agnostic among them conclude, the prophets knew no more than anybody else. If Paul is correct, spiritually being Jewish counts the most.

This brief conversation about the times and epochs, with no specific answer about the restoration of kingdom glory to the ethnic nation of Israel, as constituted under Moses, is a little puzzling for another reason. Later, when the Jewish defender Saul of Tarsus was converted by Christ and turned into the Apostle Paul, who wrote more than half of the New Testament Scriptures, it seems that time had come for God to reveal the "times and the epochs". When Paul wrote to the largely non-Jewish Christians in Thessalonica, he told them that they did not need for him to teach them about the times and the epochs, because they already knew. Between the calling of the Apostle Paul and his Epistles, it was the will of God to allow Christians to know much, but not all, about how things would turn out for the Jews.

A Christian understanding and interpretation of the ancient Hebrew prophets leads to a certainty that the prophets really were communicating the truth, and that they were not mistaken. This raises eyebrows among those who want the Holy Spirit to always speak in ordinary prose and never use apocalyptic language. Nevertheless, the Gospel of Christ went out from Jerusalem and has made it to the far corners of the nations. While literal physical Jerusalem has not been the centerpiece of the awe of the nations, and Messiah instead reigns from heaven on the Throne of David at the Right Hand of the Father, instead of physically from the earthly City of modern Jerusalem, it is still true that the prophets spoke correctly, if we think of the true permanent Temple of the New Covenant as Christians. The spiritual kingdom of God is made real among the nations by God living in the hearts of His people who trust and love His Son.

CHRISTIANS READ REVELATION TWENTY TOO SOON

The 20th Chapter of the Book of the Unveiling of Jesus Christ as Conquering King over all nations is almost universally agreed to be the part of our Christian sacred writings that is the most filled with truth expressed in dramatic and symbolic picture language of all of the writings in Holy Scripture. This reality is cited by many Christians as the reason why they are uncomfortable with this Book and uncertain that any scholar can actually get it right! This book of heavenly visions, battles, beasts, bowls of wrath, four horsemen, and candlesticks borrows images from more than a few Old Testament prophets. The message was aimed primarily at giving encouragement and strength to the persecuted First Century Christians living in seven different cities in Asia Minor, which we are told is Modern Turkey. There is a statement included in the personal word to each of the seven churches which seems to make it for all Christians everywhere, "let him that has ears hear what the Spirit says to the churches". Understanding the Book of the Revelation of Jesus Christ requires taking the time to trace the apocalyptic images used, and to examine first what is clear. There is no reference in the Bible to a period of "a thousand years" anywhere else, except in Revelation Chapter 20. This should be a red flag about reading it literally.

What is clear in this inspired writing? The unmistakeable message of the opening verses is that the things revealed in this writing must shortly come to pass, for the "time is near". Clarity begins with recognizing that the writer is not speaking about events far into the future from the writing of the Book. To miss that, or to ignore that message, seems to invite every irresponsible twist of human imagination!

So, what about the 20th Chapter? In this chapter, Christ reigns with His saints for a thousand years, while satan is locked up in prison for a thousand years. The first thing that deserves to be noticed is that this probably should fit with the opening verses of the writing. In other words, if the things revealed were about to take place when the churches received their copies of these visions, then the phrase "a thousand years" is most likely NOT referring to a literal long period of time. The only other use of the phrase "a thousand years" in the New Testament is found in Second Peter 3:8. In this verse, it is said that one is as a thousand years and a thousand years is as one day, with the Lord. The point seems to be that time is no barrier to the certainty that will always make sure that He achieves what He promised. If we apply the Apostle Peter's use of a thousand years to the Revelation, then reading a thousand years as a long time is not at all a necessity! It is just as accurate to read it as a very short time. Sadly, three different popular modes of Bible prophecy interpretation read the phrase "a thousand years" as a very long period of time. I believe this is one big factor for why the subject of the time of the end remains so controversial among Christians of all traditions and backgrounds. We read the 20th Chapter of the Revelation too soon! In other words, the words that are written in ordinary language throughout the New Testament should form the foundation of how we read the more difficult language. We know this principle, but we are not following it when it comes to the phrase "a thousand years".

Christ taught a lesson about binding the strong man, in order to plunder his house. He came to bind the strongman, satan, and plunder the kingdom of darkness. His ministry and that of His Apostles in the First Century achieved that purpose of getting the church and the Gospel kingdom planted into all nations of the known world. Satan was helpless to keep the infant Christian church from emerging and coming to be active throughout the world. These plainer words of the New Testament ought to be used to help us get a picture on what is likely meant by the phrase "a thousand years" in Revelation 20. We should not first decide our view of the phrase, and then, build our interpretation around that phrase. Rather, we should consider whether the phrase is linked directly to Christ's words about His plundering of satan's kingdom during the Gospel ministry of His visitation and the commission of His First Century Apostles.

OUR LORD'S UNIQUE BODILY RESURRECTION

Jesus conquered death for all who would ever trust in His Name. He achieved this victory over the death that the first Adam had brought, so that there is forgiveness of sins and eternal life freely given to those who call upon Him from a heart transformed by true faith in His saving death and His resurrection. The resurrection of Christ in exactly the same body that he had when He was crucified is often preached as an "example" of the bodily resurrection of Christian people in general. But, is that a Biblical idea? Is that true? Did the bodily resurrection of Jesus set a pattern of some kind for all believers? Here's why I do not think that is an accurate way to think about the uniqueness of Christ's physical resurrection.

The Authorized Version states Psalm 16:10 this way, "Thou wilt not leave my soul in hell. Neither wilt thou suffer thine Holy One to see corruption." This reference is part of the sermon preached by the Apostle Peter after the outpouring of the Holy Spirit on the Day of Pentecost, recorded in Acts 2. It is explained by Peter after quoting King David that the ancient beloved king was not speaking about himself, but his Seed, Jesus. This was a special promise that God would not allow the body of His Son to deteriorate. If it were the norm for all believers in all ages to be raised in bodies that had not fallen to deterioration, it would not have required a special promise! It was unique because it only applied to the Christ, the Seed of David, the Messiah. It was a promise of a uniqueness granted to Christ that was never promised to any other human being.

The overwhelming majority of persons who physically die experience the decay of their remains. We have some amazing preservations of some of the Egyptian mummies, so that DNA can now be obtained, in some cases. But, their bodies are still no longer something that would be regarded as feasible for use to carry on the normal functions of being naturally alive. This is because the unique promise to the Seed of King David was not given to anybody else in any other time or place. We can expect our bodies to deteriorate after we leave this world.

Why did God give a prophecy that the body of Jesus would not suffer decay? What purpose did it serve? It was useful, in one sense, as evidence of fulfillment of prophecy. For the First Century Jews, it should have been persuasive that He was the Holy One of Israel. It did help the ones who believed in His Name and received baptism that day. But, much of the nation was hardened. Nevertheless, if it were normal for the bodies of the dead to come back to life without deterioration, it would not have been unique.

The first letter to the Christians at First Century Corinth from the Apostle Paul includes a lengthy treatise on the subject of resurrection in the 15th Chapter. In these verses, it is striking that what the Holy Spirit inspired the Apostle to write seems to be ignored by most who follow tradition. Far from teaching the Corinthians that their physical remains will be reactivated, Paul emphatically tells them that a new spiritual body will emerge from the grave for all Christian believers! A natural body is placed into the grave and a spiritual body comes out. It's fairly plain speech. It's truly a "bodily resurrection", but it's not a display of the physical leftovers that we used in this life at all. No, we are not promised to be raised as our Lord was, in the sense of how the physical body is raised. We are, in fact, raised in Him, spiritually, and we are equipped with a body fitted for eternal usefulness in our resurrection. Some would argue that the Christian resurrection was the transformation of Israel out of her Old Testament Age state into the New Jerusalem Israel of God with her fullness as the Israel of God manifest forever.

THE SPECIAL PREVIEW OF THE COMING OF THE SON OF MAN

Peter, James and John were privileged to experience a special preview of the majesty of the Lord Jesus in His coming years before it took place. They were the three disciples chosen by Jesus to accompany him to the Mount of Transfiguration. There they saw the Lord become very bright and they saw Him accompanied by Moses and Elijah. Peter offered to build a tabernacle for Moses, Elijah, and Jesus, but discovered that this was not the point of the amazing experience. Later, as an Apostle, Peter wrote about this in Second Peter 1:16, referring to the event as Christ's coming in power. The Apostle Peter saw this special event as an eyewitness account of the coming of Christ in power, which is why there are scholars who tell us that there are many comings of Christ. Also, many Christian preachers and teachers see the Transfiguration as the complete explanation for the controversial words preceding it, found in the last two verses of the 16th Chapter of the Gospel of Matthew. Jesus told Peter, James and John not to mention what they saw on the Mount of Transfiguration until after His resurrection.

The Transfiguration is connected in a direct way to the words of our Lord Jesus Christ when He said "there are some standing here who will not taste death until you see the Son of Man coming in His kingdom". But, it cannot be the complete fulfillment. Included in the things that Jesus said that some of them would experience before their natural death was that Christ would come in the glory of the Father with the angels and reward every one for what they have done. The main work of the Apostles was to go and teach all nations, baptizing them into the name of the Father, and of the Son, and of the Holy Spirit. This work had not yet begun yet, let alone been completed for their lifetimes. So it was that it makes sense that the fulfillment of Christ's words was intended to be well beyond the important preview of His coming provided to three Apostles on the Mount of Transfiguration, yet still within the natural lifetime of some of His First Century followers. A "coming" in modern history fails the test.

Those who see the coming of the Son of Man in power as fulfilled in the Transfiguration are witnesses that it is not a requirement of being faithful Christians to demand that this expression has a still unfulfilled future meaning. The Transfiguration as the fulfillment of the coming of the Son of Man raises questions that are difficult to avoid. Most Christians desperately want to insist that the coming of the Son of Man is an event that is supposed to end civilization and human history. In this regard, without realizing it, Christianity is explaining the unfolding of the last days in a very similar manner to Islam, as well as to the Jewish expectation of the "End of Days". But, Christianity has a message that is far, far more positive than Islam, Judaism, or any other view of life, religious or secular! Yet, by insisting upon dogmatizing an eternally unfulfilled coming of the Son of Man, we are too often reducing the glory of the message of Christ and His kingdom committed to us. This is not an intentional Christian sin, but still, a reality!

The coming of the Son of Man which fits the timeframe that our Lord plainly placed upon fulfillment of His words is, of course, the judgment that ended the Old Covenant system of worship by the passing away of the Jewish temple and the City of First Century Jerusalem. The "coming" of Jesus was the event that established the remnant of First Century Jews, (those who believed the Good News preached by the Apostles of Jesus Christ) and the Gentile believers engrafted into Israel through faith in the Good News, as the true and Permanent Temple of God forever. The Church, the Wife of the Lamb, Christians, the daughters and sons of Abraham and Sarah by faith in the Lord Jesus the Seed of Abraham, was made secure in their covenant with God. All Israel was saved at the coming of Christ when physical and earthly and ethnic Jerusalem was fully replaced by the New Jerusalem coming down from heaven.

THE FIRST CENTURY APOSTASY FROM ACTS 20

The Apostle Paul left the City of Ephesus in tears. He was sad because he knew that something divisive and evil was about to occur. All of the Apostles of Christ had to deal false teachers constantly seeking to lure the disciples away from solid faith. But, the part that was going to happen soon, as the Apostle left Ephesus, was some of the leaders trusted by the Christians were going to leave the Faith without leaving the church. They would use their positions of trust and authority among Christians to introduce many serious and even gross departures from the teachings received from the Apostles. They would gladly betray the Apostles and even Christ Himself for whatever their various personal motives might be.

Christians have called this phenomena "apostasy". Sooner or later, the enemies of Christianity would realize that their most effective strategy to try to destroy the Christians was to pretend to be one of them, speak their language, get to know them, and use this relationship to pull them away from the truth. The lies that they desired to sell required that they start out with the same confession as the believers themselves. It was knowledge of this reality of a major falling away from true faithfulness to the teachings and ethical principles given to the church by Jesus and the Apostles that saddened the Apostle Paul very much. He was a realist. He knew this moral and spiritual tragedy was going to take place. It was a certainty. It was even necessary, in order for the true leaders to stand out. But, it still hurt a great deal to know that some who seemed like real brothers in Christ would turn out to be nothing more than serpents and Judas Iscariots!

It is very important to note that the falling away which the Apostles spoke of pertained to events in the First Century, effecting the churches that they had established and nourished in the Lord. They were not speaking of church movements hundreds or thousands of years away at all! Now, we know as students of history that the early errors that crept into the churches had longterm impact. There is much that is false that has become ingrained into the life of the church as an institution. Most of these serious errors are exaggerations of the sinfulness common to man. But, when reinforced by church leaders who are led by an agenda of undermining the Biblical message, the abuses of truth are devastating!

The Apostle John also spoke of the presence of anti-christs as clear evidence that they were living in the last hour of history. History, from the standpoint of the Biblical ages, is primarily divided into that which was driven by the Law of Moses, and was a governmental, ethnic, and tribal judicial system, as well as the worship system in the Temple, on the one side, and the coming in of the kingdom of God through Christ, on the other. During the time of the Apostles, the last days were occurring for the system that was obsolete, at the same time as the everlasting Gospel kingdom was invading satan's kingdom of darkness, to gather the First Century foundation of the Gospel believing Jews and Gospel believing Gentiles who were united by the baptism of the Holy Spirit into the true Temple of God. So, the last hour of the old and dying system or order was characterized by those who left the church, and spread philosophies that effectively set out to ruin Christians, deceive them, and harm the new Faith.

The great falling away has often been spoken of many Christians as something that has taken place in modern times. It is supposed that there was a long period when a stable supply of Christians in unity took place until the modern time. This is really false. Right when the Apostles were still alive and active, those who desired to ruin the development of Christianity led many away from the Faith. Some denied Christ under persecution, but others dropped out of the Christian race due to lies taught to them by the men who were granted the trust and opportunity to serve in leadership positions.

BELOVED IT IS THE LAST HOUR

The Apostle John wrote these words (recorded in the second chapter and verse 18) of his general epistle to Christians living in the First Century. He told them that they were living in the "last hour". He went on to explain to them that the presence of many antichrists trying to deceive them, and pull them away from straightforward Christian teaching, was evidence that they were living in the last hour. They were living in a time in human history when the world was about to pass away, and Christ would replace that world with something much better. What was passing away in the First Century? It could not have been the physical world of nature and sunlight and orbits and seasons, etc. It had to be something else.

Their circumstances as predominantly Jewish Christians was about to change for the better very soon. In historical time, it was only "hours away". They were heading into a new frontier when there would be no need to flee from the persecutions of fellow Jews from city to city. That hour was upon them. They would soon enjoy the presence of God through Christ in a new way, without being kicked out of the synagogue. They would soon meet without being hounded by their countrymen and turned over to the Romans.

The last hour for these First Century saints was a tense and unique time. We are NOT living in the last hour in our day. It's been over since that First Century change from the conflict among the Jews about whether Jesus was actually Messiah brought about an end to the Old Covenant Age (or world).

The Old Covenant Age was sentenced to pass away when our Lord gave Himself as the Perfect Sacrifice for the sins of the people at Calvary. Yet, the Age was not then ended. The beginning, or "first days", of the New Testament Age (or world), occurred at the same time as the last days of the Old Testament Age. For about forty years, the two ages collided in a major way, with the Roman Empire very much in the mix. The Roman Empire continued on past the last hour of the Old Covenant Jewish Age for three more centuries, but it was forced to succumb to the influence of the rise of the Christians, too!

Christians were fully integrated as the New form of Israel when the Old Covenant Jewish Age ended. From that point on, to be Christian was to neither be a Jew nor a Gentile, as far as spiritual heritage. This was because believing in the Jewish Messiah transforms people into sons and daughters of Abraham. As of the new start, after the last hour spoken of by the Apostle John, all persons who love God through Christ and who love another as brothers and sisters in the Christian Faith are distinctly citizens of the kingdom of God, without any need to have an ethnic pedigree. Whether your ancestors were from the ancient Hebrew tribes, or the tribes of Africa, or the tribes of any other place in this world, was irrelevant, as far as being able to be real children of Abraham.

God had promised Abraham to make his descendants more numerous than the stars of heaven! He has fulfilled this promise, and continues to fill this promise, as many millions of human beings receive Christian baptism into the covenant given to all who trust in Jesus Christ. The churches celebrate the fact of God's fulfillment of His promise to the ancient Patriarch Abraham by baptism. The churches also express the fact that we participate in the Presence of Christ Who is Lord over heaven and earth, when we share in the breaking of the Bread and drinking of the Cup. Prior to the last hour, this was the church's witness to the expectation of the return in Presence of their Lord from heaven. Since the last hour in the First Century, Christ eats and drinks with His gathered disciples as they celebrate His Presence in all places of the world, and with all believers who are already in heaven.

THE NATURE OF THE RETURN OF CHRIST

An elder in a Reformed church explained briefly to me his view of the return of Christ. He was in agreement with the late Dr. R.C. Sproul, Sr. that the coming in judgment upon First Century Jerusalem was "a coming of Christ", but he was equally certain that it could not be "the return of Christ". His opinion is shared by quite a few teachers in the Reformed Faith, including Dr. Kenneth Gentry, and Dr. Bruce W. Gore, to name only a few. These men are quite solid and capable Bible teachers, by the way.

One of the main arguments for the elder who spoke with me just before the worship time at church was the words of the angels recorded in the 8th verse of the 1st Chapter of the Acts of the Apostles. The angels told the disciples that Jesus would return in the same manner as they saw Him ascend into heaven. To the elder who spoke with me, this required an appearing that was bodily and visible, since Christ was taken up out of their sight in bodily form, and was visible until He disappeared into the cloud.

I have reasons to question the view of this elder and those who share the same understanding of the nature of the return of Christ. Christ ascended in a cloud, so His return would be in a cloud. That can be established as common ground. That it would require that everyone actually witness His coming back in a cloud is not as certain to me as it is to Christians like this elder. So, we share together the nature of Christ's return as a cloud-coming, but we do not share the idea of universal visibility to the natural eyes of all people on earth everywhere. That is significant. If he is not correct in assuming that Christ must be seen by all people everywhere in His return from heaven in the clouds, then it is very well within the framework of Christ's own words about His return to see it as a First Century event. Let me explain.

The only Bible verse that tells the reader that "every eye shall see Him" is in the context of the 1st Chapter of the Book that Unveils Jesus as the Conquering King over all nations. The earliest verses of the Revelation (or Unveiling) of Jesus Christ tells the reader that the events to be revealed "must shortly come to pass", followed up by the words "for the time is near". These events which would unveil Jesus were about to happen when they were written by John on the Isle of Patmos. That is crucial to being a fair-minded interpreter of the Book of the Revelation. In the last chapter of this Unveiling of Christ, our Lord's words are repeated five times, "I am coming soonSome Christians are convinced that John received the visions of the Unveiling in the mid-60s A.D. during the reign of Caesar Nero. Liberals and dispensationalists dogmatically insist that he wrote this Book later, when Domitian was the Roman Emperor. Either way, the same principle ought to be applied, which is that the events that were revealed took place within a short time of the Book being sent to the seven churches in Asia Minor (what is today Turkey). In other words, the timing of the events revealed was not directly going to be about the centuries much later in history from the writing of the Book.

In verse 7, John records that "every eye shall see Him, including them that pierced Him". This is the only passage in the entire Bible that tells anyone that Christ's coming will be universally visible. Consider the context. Who would be "them that pierced Him"? Nobody living in modern times directly is guilty of having pierced the Lord Jesus. We have often spoken of a spiritual sense in which we are all guilty before God, because the forgiveness of our sins required the shed blood of Christ. But, the specific inclusion of them that pierced Him as seeing His coming in the clouds makes much more sense of directing the reader toward the events of the First Century coming in judgment upon Jerusalem! The tribes of the Land of Israel mourned when they witnessed the destruction Jesus warned about 40 years earlier.

THE LOVE OF THE TRUTH IS NOT A POPULARITY CONTEST

The Apostle Paul commanded young pastors who he appointed to the office of bishop in the First Century to be diligent students of the Scriptures. This would enable them to answer the questions of both the Christians who came into the churches, as well as those outside of the churches who had honest questions about the Christian Faith. The Apostle Peter also instructed Christians to learn how to give an answer to every person who desired to know about the Christian hope. This was regarded by the Apostles as an important part of being citizens of the kingdom of God.

The love of the truth is not a popularity contest. When Christians fail to challenge unbiblical movements that arise in each new generation, this is harmful to the spiritual health of the followers of Christ, and it is a hindrance to the credibility of our common testimony before the world of the non-believing. It is no shame to be unable to prove everything that we believe. We know this because some things that God has revealed are reinforced by internal spiritual means. For example, the Apostle Paul told the believers in First Century Rome that the Holy Spirit tells our spirit that we are the children of God. That is not something that can be objectively verified, but it can still be reasonably explained to inquirers.

"Orthodoxy" is something which has value, but can easily be abused in the churches. For example, it matters a great deal when defining what we Christians call the "Incarnation". Our Lord became flesh and blood in time and history through the Virgin Mary, lived without sinning, worked genuine miracles, was crucified under Pontius Pilate, rose up bodily from the dead, commissioned His apostles to plant churches throughout the known world, ascended into the heavens, and is our Final Judge. These are "orthodox" truths. Too often, in order to claim uniquely orthodox status as a church group, people of some traditions make a series of lists that have nothing to do with basic Christian teachings, per se. They use the length of their history as an organization as evidence that they are the true church. This can be somewhat intimidating to many persons who do not know the Bible, but it's less than fair.

Sadly, many theologians who were accused of being heretics for less than Biblical reasons in history are today gladly willing to do the same thing to Christians who they teach things that they cannot disprove in an open, public, honest, fair-minded, and unprejudiced examination of the Holy Scriptures. This is a reflection of the ease with which something of universal Christian value, like the word "orthodoxy", can be made into a partisan religious weapon to satisfy a lust to use cheap political tactics to win a fight.

One example of this certainly in the teaching of the Biblical last days. The major views that are presently accepted among Christians in churches throughout the world all have their roots in the church fathers. None were well-developed at all well into the first four centuries of the Christian Faith among all nations. The least popular view has been what is often called "preterism". Most teachers of the subject of Bible prophecy use the fact of past fulfillment to get by, then run away from it, because they know it's not popular. If you absolutely deny all past fulfillment, then you are calling Jesus Christ a total liar. If you admit that much of the Bible's prophetic events, or even all, are true, then you stand in jeopardy of being treated as a persona non grata among those who value popularity.

THE RICH IN THE LAST DAYS OF JAMES CHAPTER 5

This final chapter of the Epistle of James has somewhat to say about the last days and the coming of the Lord. The opening verses expose the rich who hold back the wages of laborers in their fields. Those who James is writing to who are guilty of this evil practice are not only condemning themselves morally and spiritually before their Maker, Who will take vengeance, but they are also wasting their own greed! They are told that they are saving up riches for the "last days". This would seem to be much more than hyperbole. Something is about to take place in the near future for these rich men which will wipe out their wealth and leave them as penniless as the people who work for them! It is incumbent upon any among them who are wise to re-think how they spend their fortunes in an economy that does not have future.

The economy of First Century Jerusalem was destined to be ruined exactly as the Lord Jesus pronounced upon it, as we read in Matthew 23. So, anybody who thought of counting on possessions stored up for many years to come was not making a wise financial decision. It was wrong to cheat people out of their wages. But, it was also stupid, considering the fact that these rich men were living in the last days. This is why they were told to "weep and howl". If all that matters to a person is the "stuff" that one collects, then the guaranteed disappearance of that material blessing ends any good reason to be happy at all.

The persons who were trying to make it and were the likely objects of the abusive rich of the First Century Jewish economy were given comfort to expect relief from "the coming of the Lord".

(It could hardly seem like relief to the problems that they faced at time in the First Century if the coming of the Lord to punish their oppressors was not going to happen for thousands of years in the future!) These reminders woven into so many books of the New Testament that God was testifying to First Century Christians that help was on the way, and even "at the door", cannot be ignored without negative consequence! We do well to realize that God was telling hurting people something practical, not some pie-in-the-sky theory about a resolution of the ultimate issues of the human dilemma for all creatures at the end of all aspects of human civilization. Quite to the contrary, James is encouraging suffering Christians with promises that they are going to find real relief from their oppression in their day and age! Also, those who abuse others just because they can are about to taste some of their own medicine and lose the very thing that they love and worship more than all else: their wealth!

The whole Book of James could easily be described as the "New Testament Book of Proverbs". The teaching of this wonderful writing has aroused much discussion among Christians. It challenges the smugness of any Christian who thinks that simply being capable of explaining justification by grace through faith is a sufficient foundation for assurance. James boldly testifies that faith without works is dead. He teaches his listeners about the fiendishness of the human tongue in pretty strong language that has not been said in that way very often!

James is quite a prophetic preacher, like the great ones of the Old Testament, and even much like the Lord Jesus Christ, Himself! James is wasting no words to confront what needs to be confronted in the church. He addresses the sin of partiality, wherein it was happening that some were showing preference to well to do worshippers over poor people when the church assembled. He told them to knock it off. He was obviously a no-nonsense leader! And, so it is that he also warned them that they were living at that time in history in the Biblical last days, and that they could expect the Lord soon Who was "at hand".

WOE TO
THE CHRISTIAN "EXPERTS"

It is understood very well why we have high standards before a person is hired to operate on people with brain tumors. It's not so much about giftedness or talent, some of which cannot be quantified. It is more about professional accountability to be trusted as a skilled surgeon. The specialized degree or board certification provides relief to all parties concerned, even though we might readily admit that there could be persons in our culture who possess the wherewithal to perform brain surgeries to the highest level of excellence as the very best in the neurosurgical profession, even though they lack the necessary "paperwork" to legally apply that craft. To us, it matters that a human being is granted "orthodoxy".

This matters a great deal to the majority of the consumers of the Christian Faith, as well. Churches ordain leaders to serve as spiritual guides and "technicians", so to speak, of the craft of helping people understand God in accord with the Christian understanding. Most are persons who are doing this kind of work because they truly believe that it is of real advantage to the wellbeing of others. Some, no doubt, have other motivations. But, in Christianity, these are the ones who millions of followers of God through Christ everywhere regard as especially equipped to provide honest answers to Bible questions.

For all who give themselves to the study of the Scriptures, with a living passion to bless others, it is good and reflects well upon the advance of the kingdom of God in this world, that they are serving God and others. Those who would never, ever, ever deliberately tell a lie about the meaning of a Bible passage are true servants of the kingdom of God, and we should all be glad that they have been ordained by some church group, in order to have the benefits of an open door to serve.

For all who are little more than religious politicians, who twist the meaning of plain Bible words in order to sell books or please man or avoid criticism when some part of the Bible is not very popular, shame on them! Woe to them. They are granted social status as gurus and experts by large numbers of Christians, but they abuse that position, because they are not intellectually ethical. They want to be popular more than they care about the impact upon those who are hindered from serving God by their negligence.

This is not intended as a reason to distrust persons who serve as elders, or pastors or presbyters or bishops, or other designated areas of Christian service. It is a pleasure, in fact, that the field of theology has the input of large numbers of persons from a wide variety of traditions, who are dedicated to giving their lives to Scripture and theology. In Christian circles, the practicing theologian might be the closest thing to the constitutional law professor, or judge.

The similarities to the effort to faithfully interpret the Holy Scriptures and the effort to faithfully interpret the Constitution of the United States are significant, in my opinion. In both cases, it is possible to have a high regard for the authority of the respective subject to which the scholar is called to interpret, and yet, have vast differences regarding the most responsible principles of interpretation. Just as it is true that an ordinary Christian can often read the Scriptures as faithfully or more faithfully than a Christian theologian, so a dedicated patriotic citizen might be more faithful than a constitutional lawyer.

Nevertheless, we all benefit from the fact that the Scriptures are translated into common languages by scholars who are experts in the original languages, textual comparisons, and who offer that special skill. So the point of pronouncing a woe to the Christian experts here is not to reduce our respect for scholarship at all, but to rebuke the laziness and unethical partisanship of those who avoid the plain words of the Bible because they fear unpopularity and lower book sales, rather than being honest before God and faithful interpretations of the Scriptures that honor the privilege of their Christian calling.

ARE CHRISTIANS FOLLOWING
THE JEWISH MISTAKE?

If our New Covenant Christian Faith is the true belief system from God to save mankind from the perils of our sins and its consequences, then the Christian analysis of First Century history is that the majority of the Jewish nation made a mistake about Who Jesus really Was and Is. This is not anti-Semitism at all, but simply logic! If our spiritual inheritance from Christ and His Apostles is correct in its affirmation that God sent Jesus into the world to be the Savior of sinners, then anyone who did not recognize Him was mistaken. It is not to single out the First Century Jewish nation, except that He came primarily for them. If we who trust in His Name are right to do so, then an error took place when His ethnic people rejected Him. Of course, if the Apostles, all of whom were Jewish, were mistaken, then Christianity is false. It is just about that straightforward, and it is not easy to come up with any other reasonable explanation.

Are Christians doing something very similar to what our Jewish neighbors have done? Are we locked in a form of eschatological unwillingness to face the implications of fulfilled Bible prophecy? If so, what will be the consequences? It is worth asking the question, when it comes to loving God and leaving the last days behind. On this subject, our unwillingness to challenge ourselves places us in the awkward position of appearing to be more cynical about what Jesus and His First Century disciples taught than atheists!

What was the big mistake of the majority of the First Century Jewish nation? It was the unwillingness to consider the possibility that Jesus was, indeed, the true Messiah, for whom they had waited for in the amazing journey of their entire history. From the promise of the Almighty to Eve that the Seed from her womb would crush the head of the serpent, to the promise of Moses that a leader like him would be granted to Israel, to the belief that there would arise One to rule from the Throne of David, all of these powerful prophecies and hopes were dismissed, because of what their natural minds craved. The First Century Jewish leaders contended between zealots who wanted to revolt and overthrow the indignity of Roman servitude and those in high political power who wanted to preserve the power connection with the Roman Establishment. In both cases, only a leader who would deliver from Roman domination would be acceptable. Thus, they missed their visitation, if the Christians are on the right track.

Christians, by and large, refuse to take seriously what the Lord Jesus said about the purpose of the coming of the Son of Man to reward His First Century disciples and establish the everlasting kingdom. It is common for most Christians to dogmatically insist that Jesus did NOT come back in the First Century! In fact, if any Christian challenges this dogma, that person is often accused of heresy without a trial! Why is this? It is because of the erroneous opinions in our natural thinking about what the "Second Advent" ought to look like. So, we disregard the impact of our Savior's own words, as recorded in the Gospels, and of the words in the pastoral epistles, and the admonition from Jesus that His coming would be very soon in the first and last chapters of the Book of the Revelation! We go out of our way to take the strength out of the plainest language in the whole Bible, in order to oppose the truth that the last days were finalized exactly when the Lord Jesus promised that it would happen.

Like our Jewish neighbors, we Christians stubbornly set our minds on earthly visions of the kingdom of God that cloud our ability to reason through the Bible on its own terms. This compels us to react to the tendency of liberals to over-allegorize by refusing to rely upon allegory when it is most definitely the only way to rightly discern the meaning of passages! At the same time, by refusing to consider the possibility that Christ's words mean what they plainly appear to be saying, we also disrespect the professed appreciation for "literal, historical and grammatical context" which many, especially Protestants, claim as vital tools of reading the Bible. May the Lord help us overcome this error.

THE SOCIAL PSYCHOLOGY
OF THE LAST DAYS

Christians are spiritually nurtured in fellowships where there is the substantial truths of the message that binds all true believers from all generations, races, and places. Yet, it is equally true that all of us who come to love God and our fellow Christians are influenced by the culture within our own groups, much as we are in our households and neighborhoods and schools. In other words, there can be an overlap of the substance of what we have in common with the stuff from the assumptions that we add to that substance, in order to be a distinct group. As an example, you can ask a devout Catholic, devout Lutheran, devout Presbyterian, devout Methodist, devout Church of Church member, devout Baptist, or devout Pentecostal the question, "Is Jesus Christ truly the Savior of sinners?", and you will either be given a "yes" or that individual is deliberately denying something essential to what their professed church allegiance claims! There is no variance to the answer from these professing Christians, in spite of many big differences.

Within each of the above listed groups, however, there is a "psychology", in my opinion, that both members within these church groups, and observers of these church groups can either readily identify, or at least, say "oh, yeah, that's right", when they hear about it. For example, a person who attends a Roman Catholic mass on a regular basis, along with many people from Orthodox churches and Episcopal churches, will stand out from Baptists and most Protestants by the "sign of the Cross". This is a practice that grew up in church history, some say spontaneously. While it is not looked upon by either side as a major reason to be alienated from each other at all, we notice it. This is mentioned. not as a problem for people, but simply as part of the psychology of inter-church relationships, where one person will say, "he or she is probably Catholic or Orthodox or Episcopal", when they see them using their hand to make the sign of the Cross. All of us understand that the psychology of our environments influence us.

I was involved for some years in a church fellowship within the Pentecostal and Charismatic persuasion. The folks from this background today do not use the same special language of the psychology of these groups that was not uncommon in my youth. At that time, when I attended, it was not unusual to hear a person of Pentecostal persuasion ask, "Don't you believe in the Holy Spirit?" to someone in a dialogue about what signs indicate that a Christian is filled with the Holy Spirit. In many churches, pastors would cringe when they heard this, because most fully agreed with non-Pentecostal Christians that every person who has been born of God by the power of the Holy Spirit through faith in Christ possesses the indwelling of the Holy Spirit. But, it was not unusual to hear questioning of someone as believing or not believing in the Holy Spirit, mistakenly said as sort of part of the psychology of our group connection. It was not that most pastors held to that, but what was taught seemed to produce that psychology.

The universal church everywhere in all places and languages and generations proclaims with unity and certainty the absolute fact that Jesus Christ and the Apostles taught with no apology His return from heaven, or the "Second Advent", as Christians have often called it. The fact of the Second Coming is an essential truth of the revelation of the Holy Scriptures that cannot be denied without the same effect as the person who answers "is Jesus Christ truly the Savior of sinners?" with any other answer but "yes". But, this universal Christian confession is modified with adjectives that impose a very different set of things which are then translated into the psychology of the last days that unfairly ridicules past fulfillment.

We should demand that we separate the FACT of the universal Christian confession of the Second Advent from the misleading abuse of that FACT which happens when we superimpose the adjectives "future, physical, and visible", which are unfair ways in which the psychology of the last days tries to force a Christian to make a fraudulent choice. "Do you believe in the Second Coming?" is supplanted by a demand that you must believe in what amounts to a denial of Christ's own words. "Don't you believe in the Second Coming?" is an absolute "yes" by all serious Christians, but not with unfair adjectives!

Why is this a serious matter? It is because of what is well understood among Christians from all kinds of church traditions. The issue that makes it extremely difficult for most Christians, regardless of how persuasive the Biblical reasons, to ever admit that the coming of the Son of Man was a First Century event, is due to the strong desire that all real Christians have for unity in the Christian essentials. Here we have to be able to do more than draw a mere technicality out of a hat and call it "orthodoxy". We have to be brutally honest with ourselves about why words are rejected as meaning what they say by people who would not do such a thing with most other areas of the Bible. What causes the willingness of most Christians to deny the plain meaning of words when it comes to the Second Advent?

I think we can see how that the psychology of the whole subject of the last days and the subject of the coming of the Son of Man has been treated unfairly over the centuries. Whenever people, even devout Christians, feel threatened, we find ourselves tempted to use arbitrary means to explain away what seems like a contradiction in the words of the Bible. It is a mistake made by millions to try to protect the Bible and the Lord Jesus from the appearance of making a mistake. It is no more necessary nor helpful than when ancient Lot offered to give his daughters to the perverts of Sodom, in order to save the angels visiting him at his house! It was done under duress, but was still not the choice that pleased God.

Christians are duped into a false choice by pastors (most of whom are probably well-meaning), by the effects of the psychology of the talk of the last days upon our ability to discuss the Biblical last days straight from the Scriptures. So it is that the believer is told by a Christian leader, "we believe in the future, physical and visible coming of Christ". The believer is thinking, "well, for sure, I have read about the Second Coming", without realizing that these are TWO SEPARATE THINGS!

Theologians, and all Christians, for that matter, have the freedom to say that they believe in the "future, physical, and visible coming of Christ". But, they absolutely do NOT have the moral and ethical right to claim that believing in these adjectives is necessary, in order to actually believe in the Christian teaching of the Second Coming of Jesus Christ! It is a very unethical demand upon the consciences of all of the people of God in Christ to make such a demand, based entirely upon terms that the person making the statement is unwilling to dispute. In other words, that leader is pretending that if you do not believe that the Second Coming of Jesus Christ is "future, physical and visible", then you have denied an essential teaching of the Lord Jesus and His holy Apostles, and you are outside of the Christian Faith on a major issue. This is grossly abusive and unfair and is absolute no different from any Pope in history telling Protestants that they are heretics because they do not believe in good works as conditions of salvation. It is arbitrary and based upon the use of adjectives which the Christian is not able to respond to.

What I have sadly learned over the past thirty years or so is that it takes remarkable courage to stay strong in defense of a Biblical reality that is unpopular socially. Truth is such a marvelous gift! To all of us who have called upon the Lord Jesus, who count our baptisms as blessings which remind us of His saving grace, we claim that He is the Truth! To have the greatest truth of the ages, the precious Word of God, politically manipulated in the way that this subject of the last days occurs, is a tragedy of shameful proportions. It is not as though such things have never occurred in history, of course. People used the Word of God to support the institution of slavery, but it was never a proper use of the Word of God, even when it was so extraordinarily popular that hardly anyone could politically survive who challenged it! So it is that every genuine scholar knows, and all Christians should admit, that there is a major difference between confessing the BIBLICAL FACT of Christ's Coming and adding adjectives that force disunity.

CAESAR NERO AND THE BIBLICAL LAST DAYS

Studies of the life of the Roman Emperor who famously fiddled while Rome burned seems to suggest that his death was the kindest contribution that he ever made to his fellow human beings. That is not a very nice thing to say about a man's life. I realize that. However, it is hard to see in what is reported to be his deeds while holding power that can bring about a different impression. He was ruthless and vicious and vain, to summarize his murders and sadistic treatment of others. Nero blamed the burning of Rome on the much despised Christians in 64 A.D. in order to shift blame away from himself. He ordered them to be burned alive at the stake night after night over a four year period. The question for people who are serious students of the Bible is whether he was the beast described in the 17th Chapter of the Book of the Revelation of Jesus Christ. Was he the man with the number 666? If so, this would be further evidence that the last days were completed in the First Century. Let's consider several items.

Much has been written about the number "666" by more than a few writers, so I'll leave it alone for this essay. Instead, the order of the kings is what I think might deserve some attention. The beast who is described is a man who is the sixth of a series of seven. If this was intended to help First Century readers gain insight into who this person actually was, as a historic figure, than we have more than a minor clue. There are some difficulties with this, because of the differences between two early Roman historians. Suetonius began his list with Julius Caesar. If we follow that list, then Nero would have been the sixth Emperor of Rome. This is not a dogmatic resolution of the matter. Yet, since the Revelation is written to deal with persecuted disciples of Jesus in the First Century, it makes sense that the first Roman Emperor to openly murder Christians in large numbers would be identified as the Beast.

The Roman Empire itself was definitely a co-conspirator with the Jewish leaders in the persecution of the Christians in the generation after Christ rose from the dead. For this reason, Jerusalem is pictured as committing adultery with the Roman Empire. From the Book of Matthew, Chapter 23, it is evident that this is Jerusalem, because Jesus in Matthew's Gospel accused Jerusalem of the blood of the prophets, and this was also true of Mystery Babylon.

So, what about Caesar Nero's role in the drama of the last days? Even without being able to argue dogmatically that he is identified in the Book of Revelation, his ugly deeds stood out so much from any of his predecessors that he should be regarded as the most notable candidate! Why does it matter? It matters because of the specifics of the order of the kings given in Chapter 17. It matters because it makes no sense that John would tell the Christians that 666 was the "number of a man", if, in fact, the idea of a specific individual human being was only symbolic of the Roman Empire in general. For these reasons, it is likely that the most corrupt Roman Emperor, who happened to follow the 5th emperor when the order listed by Suetonius is taken, is regarded as the Beast.

There has been so much speculation throughout the unfolding of the Christian Era about different dictators and political rulers with efforts to make their names fit with the number 666, as we all know. Isn't it wisest to place the greatest credibility in regard to the one historic figure who lived and ruled as a terrible man during the time when the events of the Revelation were said to be unfolding? Modern beasts of the imaginations of sensationalist preachers make no sense. They could not have been something relevant to the lives of the members of the seven churches to whom the Revelation was sent, and to whom the message was intended to help and encourage through difficult times.

THE INFORMATION AGE AND THE LAST DAYS

We live in a time that is truly fascinating, in respect to communication technology! I was born in January 1954. Most of the exposure to great ideas, for me, came from books. It was a delight to read the Bible from the King James Version many times. As I grew older and hungered for exposure to learning from the fields of science, history, political science, and religion, my visits to the local library were a healthy relief from the ordinary stresses of life during my time as a Navy hospital corpsman. I never dreamed that it would happen in my lifetime that we could learn about all of these subjects, as well as music and comedy and almost anything that entertains the human mind, from a little handheld device! We hear complaints about the distractions that are caused by the obsession of many persons with iphones, and it is not hard to see why this creates problems. But, the positive result of the modern information age is an explosion of rapid exposure to so much that is worthy to be considered and compared! Wow!

This has enormous benefit to all Christians who love the study of the Scriptures. Access to google brings discussions of a wide range of subjects. A person can study comments on every book in the Bible, as well as every word can be traced to its ancient language starting point, all at the fingertips of the average person without a college degree! The Christian can compare the different opinions of the finest scholars in history and the modern time without spending their lives in a monastery or library. Youtubes abound, free of charge, that provide an individual with solid exposure to events in the past. Yes, there is plenty of junkola on the internet. But, a discerning Christian mind can be thoroughly edified and enriched in the pursuit of the Christian goal of becoming better and better equipped to understand many subjects!

The Biblical last days can be studied now more than ever before. Any Christian so inclined can type in "The Fall of Jerusalem in 70 A.D.", for example, and a myriad of useful youtubes, some quite well done, will pop up. Debates among knowledgeable proponents of the developed interpretations within the Christian Faith are available, as well, on this subject, and many others. No modern Christian has an excuse to live in today's world with no investigation of the issues that impact our lives. The Biblical last days greatly impacts our lives. If Jesus Christ actually foretold the events that brought the devastation to First Century Jerusalem and the Temple in the Jewish revolt against the Romans, then this miraculous foretelling of the central event in Jewish history is of such a magnitude to both Judaism and Christianity, that it is almost a sin to deliberately learn nothing about it!

One of the advocates of the idea that the church is God's "world without end" is Dr. Don K. Preston. His books are produced by JaDon Management, 1405 4th Ave. N.W., Suite #109, Ardmore, Oklahoma, 73401. I mention this pastor, teacher, and author, whose messages can be accessed on the internet, because of the fact that he is wellknown among Christians who believe that it's long past due to love God and leave the last days behind. Any Christian who wants to explore this whole subject in depths would do well to contact him and order reading material. Also, he has youtubes that are very helpful. I was particularly aided in coming to grips with the meeting in the air spoken of by the Apostle Paul in his first letter to the Christians in Thessalonica by reading 'We Shall Meet Him in the Air: The Wedding of the King of kings". As is true of any two Christians anywhere in the world, I may not see eye to eye with Dr. Preston on some other matters. But, I cannot overemphasize his expertise in logically explaining this subject!

The Information Age that has come to be normal experience for many, many millions of human beings may have its down side, for sure. But, it also has a great opportunity for every single person who loves the advance of the kingdom of God. It should be regarded as a help for those who are disciplined enough to use it sensibly and wisely. Certainly, the church should use this resource for the kingdom.

LIBERALISM AND THE LAST DAYS

All of us take a few hits about our thinking if we come to the conclusion that we ought to love God and leave the last days behind. For Christians who find themselves in conservative evangelical centers of Christian fellowship, they might come to question much of the movement to promote the modern secular State of Israel as a fulfillment of the words of the Old Testament Hebrew Prophets. That is a highly popular source of best-selling novels and sensationalist preaching that puts money in the bank for many of the religious superstars in our day. But, there are also implications for Christians who have been committed to the philosophy of modern liberalism. Much (not all) of modern religious liberalism seems to be more skeptical of the authority of the Scriptures as moral and ethical guidance than those who are outright secularists! This is a weird phenomena, as far as Christian moderates and Christan conservatives can observe! There seems to be within modern religious liberalism such an animosity against anything or anyone who views the Bible as truly given by inspiration of God, and it isn't easy to explain.

Liberalism, at least, the kind which uses the Christian name to advance its goals, and works hard at injuring the trust in Scripture of ordinary believers, is something which should be re-assessed for any its circles who truly envision the King of kings as giving the world a strong foundation for knowing God. This is because, if the last days are behind us, this means that liberalism is wrong about its skeptical presumption that God did not foretell the actual future long before it happened through the prophets of the Old Testament and through our Lord Jesus Christ. Obviously, if it becomes increasingly clear that the Gospel accounts were written prior to the fall of First Century Jerusalem, then it will expose liberalism as a naked front for raw political leftwing propaganda, rather than a kingdom tool of helping people come to know God and enjoy Him, as all serious Christians hope that their time on earth contributes toward.

The last days has powerful influence, properly understood, for all Christians and all of the movements that have come about! For the cause of modern liberalism, it is not altogether fatal, if those liberals who are serious Christians acknowledge the First Century fulfillment of the last days. In fact, in the areas where classical liberalism has advanced a positive agenda of urging racial equality, respect between the genders, greater interest in the forgotten in our communities, a new vigor could actually take shape. Instead of being opponents of the authority of Scripture, Christians whose liberalism is defined within the structure of revealed Biblical wisdom will do more than shake their fists at capitalism or vague definitions of inequality. Rather, they will put direct spiritual muscle into building upon the common ground with non-liberals when it comes to really solving social problems. For example, who opposes such things as the goal of a workplace where a team spirit is obvious?

Liberalism, as a theological philosophical system, will require some modification, in order to have credibility, when most people are aware of the fact that the Bible has made remarkable, and even miraculous, claims that have been verified by secular history. Again, the contribution to the development of modern civilization in areas such as demanding that we find ways to be more inclusive of people who have felt distant from the larger society will only be enhanced by regaining a respect for the Bible!

Will it be that both the weaknesses of Zionism among popular advocates of man on the brink of a bloody modern tribulation among some on the Right, and the reduction of all of the Bible to mere allegorical lessons about how to hold hands and sing "We are the World" among liberals will be changed? I don't know. But, I can say with certainty that these results could enhance a joyful step toward Christian unity, Christian cooperation, and Christian superb reasoning, that makes me hope that all Christians will study the subject of the Biblical last days carefully, and find it profitable.

HOW IS THAT SOME BIBLE TRUTHS REMAIN MINORITY VIEWS?

My view that we should love God and leave the last days behind does not resonate with the majority of fellow Christians. Why is that? If the Biblical last days are a matter of history, what is the cause of the minority status of this view? This question deserves some straightforward answers, and I will attempt to provide them. It is not enough to write off all of the criticisms of my view. Some criticisms make a lot of sense to many people. Since my current view evolved over time, and it was not easy to affirm it for a good while after being exposed, my personal explanations for the minority status of the belief that the last days are entirely behind us include several things. The resistance includes the connection of many "dots" in Biblical literature, the vision of what the world should look like if we are in the everlasting kingdom of God right now, the confusion of the early church fathers on the subject of the last days, and the emotional need to be in the majority that humans have probably craved since the beginning.

First of all, drawing conclusions about the end of the last days is impacted by how the greatest covenant themes of the Bible fit together. What is the great covenant theme that the Bible presents to Christians from the Book of Genesis to the end of the last words in the Book of the Revelation of Jesus Christ? If we can come to some strong agreements about these questions, all Christians will be closer to a unified view of Bible prophecy. In regard to this, the building of a called out nation for Himself is one of the great themes of Scripture. From Adam to Abraham to Moses, a covenant people were being cultivated to inherit a special promise that transcended ordinary nationhood. Few evangelical scholars would disagree with this starting point. There was a set of corporate experiences for the ancient Hebrews that united them in an understanding of a unique relationship with the Creator, Redeemer and Ruler. It required testings that often brought them to sense their common destiny, which was expanded to include a lasting impact upon all nations of mankind. For the Christian, this calling culminated in the Bethlehem Event, with the life, ministry, death, resurrection, ascension, and witness to all the nations of the Lord Jesus Christ, the Jewish Rabbi Who was both the Hope of Israel and the Light to the Gentiles. He united Jew and Gentile into His New Creation, the Christian Church, and this became the fulfillment of the promise to Israel of perpetual existence as the true Israel of God. Within this Biblical outworking, there are a number of things that have to be connected, so that the Christian can understand the complete fulfillment of Old Testament prophecy in the Person of Christ and what He has brought to us.

Secondly, the language of the kingdom of God sounds so different from what many Christians see as the reality of human existence. Jesus told Nicodemus that a person cannot see the kingdom of God without being born from above. Typically, we have read that as being unable to go to heaven without receiving the spiritual birth that comes to all who belong to Christ. But, it is likely much more than that! It is likely to mean that our natural obsession with what appears to contradict the presence of the kingdom is too overwhelming for us, obscuring just how dramatic the change has been, unless and until the brightness of the transformation from before Christianity to since Christianity was planted in the world is seen by our eyes. Such a change in our eyesight probably means that history matters more than the daily news! History has a far greater impact upon carefully examining and re-examining our view of the last days than it does on absolutely any other single teaching in Christianity! Jesus told His disciples that the kingdom does not come by observation. In contrast, we find the kingdom by its effects after the fact!

The early church fathers taught some contradictory things about the kingdom, and those contradictions remain. Many acknowledged that the destruction of First Century Jerusalem was a major fulfillment of Bible prophecy, but most came short of calling it the actual "coming of the Lord" that the Apostles taught the first generation of believers to expect in their lifetime. So, because of this, the range of speculative Christian guesses about the meaning of what had occurred during the ministry of the Apostles was never widely agreed upon. This produced advocates for a literal future one thousand year reign of Christ with His saints, as well as others who read this as spiritually fulfilled in the church. These issues could not be adequately discussed, as well, because of the fact that the developing young Christian Church faced obstacles of every kind during these centuries, including the fact that their leaders were subject at any moment to the whims of those who hated them, and saw them as villainous fanatics. They did not obtain legal status in the Roman Empire for nearly three centuries following the destruction of First Century Jerusalem. This made it difficult to formulate the luxury of being able to debate the issues surrounding the last days with the kind of freedom modern Westerners now enjoy!

Finally, I think that it is very human for all of us to avoid pain. Should we discover in the Holy Scriptures something that runs contrary to the groupthink we group up with, a decision has to be made. For most of us, we then must count the social cost. If the issue does not appear to be of earth-shaking importance, then it is not going to be the case that we go against the grain of our social comfort zone. It is probably true that every single human being alive is faced with some kinds of decisions about whether to make a change, when there is a social price to be paid. Nobody who studies the interactions among Christians about Bible prophecy can possibly deny that there is a high price to be paid to challenge the popular status quo! Most sensible Christians recognize that taking a firm stand on an issue that fellow Christians find disturbing, even when it can be reasonably defended well from the Bible, is high risk behavior in much of Christian Church life! So it goes. The question for folks like me has to be, "What makes the finality of the last days in the First Century worth getting in trouble with other Christians?" Does it really matter, since I am among those who do not judge the basic sincerity of a believer's profession of Christ by whether they hold to this or that view of the last days. I came to believe it was only ethical for me to step forward and defend this view because I truly believe it has far more impact upon how we think and live than we realize. Also, it is necessary, because we are failing to defend the integrity of Christ as Prophet if we shrug our shoulders at what men see as His inability to tell the future. The disinterest in standing for the honesty and competence of Jesus as Prophet of God Who made no mistakes is something which puzzles me to observe among Christians. It is not surprising that opponents of the kingdom of God accuse Jesus of error, but it is surprising that Christians do not make any attempt to offer an answer that makes sense! Love God and leave the last days behind is part of my conviction that this issue deserves more discussion among workaday Christians, whether or not the theological and philosophical elite of the church ever do climb on board.

DEUTERONOMY 28:15-68 FULFILLED IN THE FIRST CENTURY A.D.

The law of Moses provided conditions for blessings and cursings that would determine whether or not the ancient national and ethnic Israelites could continue to possess and be blessed in their land. In their last days, the last generation of Old Covenant national and ethnic Israel and Judah, they were finally driven out by the invading Roman army, in fulfillment of the guarantees in this painful chapter. The horrible nightmarish scenes described became reality during the years of the siege of Jerusalem, according to firsthand history by Josephus. It is documented that the Jews experienced all of these terrible curses.

This is important and vital for all people to become familiar with, for several reasons. First, it was a distinctly Jewish set of specific commands with specific blessings for obedience and curses for disobedience. The Nation was called to be separate from the rest of the ancient nations. The other nations did not receive anything like the Ten Commandments, or the writings of great prophets, in the manner as ancient Israel. Ancient Israel, under the Old Covenant worship system, sacrificed physical offerings on their altar, and their center of worship was the physical City of Jerusalem, where they maintained a physical temple. All of that was given to them with many elaborate Sabbaths and other ceremonies, and special food laws, in order to make them into the distinct nation that would bring into the world the Holy One of Israel, the Savior of the world, and be the source of the world's healing.

The fact that the blessings and curses that are listed in this chapter of Deuteronomy were given to keep the Nation of Israel aware of their responsibilities, and was not given to nations around them, nor to nations that have arisen since their fall in the year 70 a.d., should not make us think that God does not actively judge all nations. Every nation is judged by God on the basis of reasonable treatment of its citizens according to what is commonly well known to be principles of sound mercy and justice. Any nation that thinks it can abuse its citizens and escape God's eye is sadly mistaken. Yet, the specific covenant tests spoken of for ancient Israel are not intended to be applied to all nations directly.

National and ethnic Old Covenant Israel became fully disobedient in their last generation, which happened to be the first generation of the New Covenant expression of the kingdom of God. The First Century was a time of transition, when the rulers of Old Covenant Israel resisted the Christ and His holy Apostles, attempting to stop the Gospel from saving people and ingrafting believing non-Jews into Israel by faith in the Lord Jesus. So the First Century was the last days of the Old Covenant system at the very same time as it was the first days of the New Covenant system for God's Israel. The Old Covenant system of a physical temple in physical Jerusalem with physical sacrifices was in the process of being permanently replaced with the New Covenant system of spiritual people in spiritual New Jerusalem gathering to offer spiritual sacrifices in every place where Christians gather. The model of the physical temple as the center of adoration to God was being fully replaced by the Christian model of the people who have been washed in the blood of Christ as the holy Temple of God forever and ever.

Wise human beings must understand that all things given to people through the sacred books of the Bible have great positive usefulness as ethical guidelines and challenges to live right. The Apostle Paul told the believers in First Century Corinth that the documentation of the destruction of those who were punished during the Exodus was an example for Christians living in the First Century, which Paul referred to as "the ends of the ages". This reminds us that we should value the lessons not be murmurers nor complainers in the church. Likewise, all Scripture teaches us much about honoring God and being true witnesses to the excellence of Jesus Christ in how we treat people, how we think, and how we live.

CALVINISM MODIFIED
BY FULFILLMENT

The general teachings of the Christian Faith that God has brought about the new birth in those who have been chosen in His Son to inherit eternal life is often nicknamed "Calvinism", because the related teachings were expounded by the French Reformer John Calvin in his famous work entitled "The Institutes of the Christian Religion". Because Pastor Calvin was gifted in logical order of clarification, this set of teachings, which he frequently acknowledged to be the important principles of the sovereignty of God, have often been treated as his opinions. As anyone who reads through the Bible will freely discover, the idea of the sovereign rulership of God is established throughout the sacred pages! Yet, many people try to make Calvin into the inventor of these great Christian truths, which is a mistake.

Nevertheless, since the word "Calvinism" is reasonably well known among professing Christians, it conveys enough commonly understood meaning to use it cautiously to describe the approach to the study of Scripture which affirms certain convictions. Among these convictions are predestination, that is, God deciding who would be called out by the Good News before they were born. Also, the teaching that the spiritual new birth in Christ accords by the miraculous work of the Holy Spirit and is absolutely independent of the natural human will. There are other convictions that can be considered, but these two are at the heart of what different followers of Jesus tend to see as problematic.

One of the reasons for the problems many people find who object to predestination and the absence of the human will in the spiritual new birth in Jesus Christ is that they think it tends to cause some people to actually blame God for their own evil conduct! Christians who gladly affirm that God predestined in eternity past disagree with the notion that His sovereign choice is the cause of human depravity. But, it has to be conceded that some people will use the idea that God is in control as an excuse. "God made me the way that I am", implies that because God has not either killed the sinner for sinning, or else, forced the sinner to live differently, then it must mean that God actually caused the rebellious deeds! That does not make sense to Christians who believe that God has complete control in all things, and who also believe just as sincerely that God, Who is perfectly righteous, is completely just in all His Being.

What does trouble me, as a Christian who could be classified as Calvinistic in relation to believing that our spiritual birth in Christ is miraculously caused by the Holy Spirit entirely apart from the natural human will, is when I witness some who are Calvinists with what seems to be anger at persons who are not Calvinists. That seems to be a contradiction of the confidence in God's outworking of His will that should be consistent with an affirmation of His governance! I hope that I never become an "angry Calvinist", which I tend to think actually flows from reading the Bible with a very negative view of the outworking of His kingdom among men, rather than actually resulting from faith in His sovereignty.

To love God and leave the last days behind, whether a professing Christian is Calvinistic, non-Calvinistic, or even anti-Calvinistic, will probably help to delete much of the grotesque religious anger from the soul, which is unhelpful. To believe that God was in Christ reconciling the world to Himself, and to believe that all who are ordained to eternal life will most certainly be saved and conformed to the image of Christ, is a thoroughly joyful foundation for life! Add to that foundation the certainty that the prayer taught by Jesus, when He said to pray "Thy will be done ON EARTH AS IT IS IN HEAVEN is being answered by God claiming many millions of people for Himself in each new generation of humanity, and you have a recipe for Christian optimism, profound joy, and no reason to be angry with those who are angry at you.

ORGANIZED CHURCHES AS THE BIBLICAL SUPREME COURT FOR MANY CHRISTIANS

The analogy can only go so far, I realize, between justices serving on the Supreme Court of the United States of America, and organized Christian churches serving as "justices", so to speak, rendering verdicts about the right meaning of the Holy Scriptures for believers in all nations and generations who sometimes find some of these decisions a blessing, and sometimes, a curse! There seems to be some basis, in my opinion, for the fact that organized Christianity in the history of the joys and struggles of Christians has had a relationship to the understanding of the kingdom of God that explains how she can be extremely important without necessarily being guaranteed that she will always get it right.

This view of the organized Christian churches differs from several Christian traditions. This view affirms that some basic Christian truths were, in fact, so deeply ingrained into the foundation of Christianity that they are preserved in all places and generations with real certainty that they are the teachings and traditions given to all sincere Christian believers by the Lord Jesus Christ and the Apostles themselves. In this category is the fact that Jesus Christ is the only Name under heaven given among men whereby we must be saved, because God was manifest in the flesh, justified in the Spirit, seen of angels, preached unto the Gentiles, believed on in the world, and received up in glory. That much of the confession of all Christians everywhere is truly catholic and undisputed by all who reverence the authority of Scripture.

What a few traditions would be hesitant to accept, but which I think sanity demands, is that there is a category of Biblical truth claims that have never been clarified enough among enough Christians in church history to be legitimately called part of true Biblical "orthodoxy". While the FACT that our Lord and His Apostles guaranteed His Second Advent, the TIMING of His coming is not the same thing! Certainly, it is self-evident that the "rulings", so to speak, of churches about how to properly interpret the prophetic writings have had advocates of a number of distinct opinions. This should give dogmatists pause who try to ostracize Christians who are teaching that we should love God and leave the last days behind. The view that the last days foretold by Jesus and His apostles came to pass in the destruction of First Century Jerusalem had many advocates among the early church fathers. Some of them also took a view of the phrase "a thousand years" that would seem to make them into one of the competing systems. The point here is that the church, by simply preserving the text of the Scriptures, and by coming to agree on the full and complete canon of the New Testament, has provided the ground of the truth, but not a unified interpretation of the ground of the truth. That means that there is still work to do to be faithful to Jesus Christ in regard to understanding, explaining, and wisely applying the prophetic Bible passages.

To love God is our first Christian duty, and with it, to love our neighbor as we love ourselves. How does a right attitude about the study of Bible prophecy fit into this Christian priority? Personally, I think it has much more than we realize to do with strengthening our worship of God in regard to our first Christian duty! Prophecy is more than a satisfaction of Christian curiosity about how we think the world might come to an end. It is far more than a debate tool to make us better at proving our debate points. It is influential to the Christian in helping us grow in grace properly, enjoy the kingdom of God, find our place of service to others, and even whether we think the world is guaranteed to get worse and worse.

To leave the last days behind is a revolutionary call for today, but it is NOT something based upon a novel idea at all! From the earliest centuries, there were church fathers who taught that the end of the

Old Covenant system in the destruction of First Century Jerusalem was a major fulfillment of Bible prophecy. What was NOT said, of course, in dogmatic language affirmed widely in the church, was this was the coming of the Son of Man in glory that He promised. By, keeping the Scriptures preserved for all Christians in all generations, the church has enabled us to read these words and not ignore them.

REJECTION OF PRETERISM AND ITS IMPACT UPON CHRISTIANITY

PAUL RICHARD STRANGE, SR   Waxahachie Texas 75165

Christians need to be able to overcome all petty divisions. There are likely to always be some divisions that amount to cultural distinctions that are good and normal. For example, if church "a" has public ministers with special robes and church "b" does not care for that, this is not something to upset folks a great deal. By contrast, the fact that atheists and religious anti-christians are not facing much opposition in the churches of the United States of America has a cause....and part of that cause is related more to Bible prophecy than we are willing to imagine. The popular views of Bible prophecy among American Christians in the last century has had a powerful effect, in my opinion, that can only be reversed by more and more Christians possessing the moral courage to study what is called "preterism"!

Preterism is dangerous, if separated from the whole of Biblical teaching: it is an incredible blessing, if studied from the vantage point of having first read through the entire Bible several times, with, hopefully, some readings in one setting of whole books of the English Bible (I am speaking here as a simple Christian whose cultural life is limited to being an American citizen without any foreign language competence). The first book in our Bible, Genesis, can be better appreciated and understood for all Christians, both as God's holy inspired Word, and as covenantal literature, if we would read it all on an afternoon, possibly, on the Lord's Day. My ability to consider an interpretation of the early chapters of Genesis that I now am persuaded fits with Scripture as a whole was facilitated by reading Genesis through in several hours, rather than just piecemeal. Others might have better ways, but I believe that this helps immensely, as something to try once, for those who preach and teach, especially!

Rejection of preterism is FAR MORE DANGEROUS than preterism in its worst extremes! Why? Because, it forces religious politics to replace Biblical reasoning, so that it becomes unacceptable in the house of God for a Christian to be honest about passages of the Bible. For example, when our Lord told His First Century disciples that He would come in His kingdom in their natural lifespan, and that their generation would not pass away until this happened, the politically correct rejection of preterism forces a lie to prevail in preaching and teaching, which cannot help but affect other areas of Christian attitude and behavior. Rejection of preterism creates the same religiously correct environment in the houses of Christian fellowship that exist politically in the larger culture, because of Leftwing Hollywood lies! Honest conversations are hard to come by in American politics because of this. It starts in church!

Preterism does not have to be fully embraced to be a major blessing to the reading of all areas of the Scriptures. Many Christians could never embrace it, regardless of how close they came, because it contradicts some things that are drilled so deeply in their psyches that it cannot respond to logic nor reason nor anything short of a miracle. But, preterism studied with as much of a fairminded attitude as a Christian pastor can come up with will reverse many things that devastate the potential good influence on the culture, including even politics, that Christians could have for the salvation of our nation! Included in these benefits would be the enormous energy toward building stronger marriage covenants, stronger family households, stronger communities, and discerning whose philosophy is most beneficial among leaders seeking our support in the public square would almost automatically follow from shifting away from a natural senses view of Christ's coming in His kingdom to one that sees Him reigning over the nations with full authority in heaven and earth. If Christians quit supposing that God has centered His prophetic word around the modern Middle East, and realize that the Great

Tribulation was the First Century Jewish-Roman War, this alone would refocus Christians on recovering our society from the pits! We can think right now and have a great nation 100 years from now!

Christians should reject fanaticism, whether preterist or anti-preterist. My own assessment at the present time is that bigotry against preterists and preterism is doing unbelievable injury to the cause of Christianity and its ability to challenge the malignant growth of anti-Christian bigotry and atheistic arrogance in an effective way. Preterism will empower and equip the people of God to think independently and to apply truth to the problems we face in Century Twenty-One. Much of what is called "conservative, Bible-believing" Christianity is just locked into unhealthy religious political correctness as what is labeled "liberalism". Why, because conservatives want a form of literalness that the Holy Spirit never inspired and liberals want to please whatever the neopagan cravings of the unbelieving elite want! Preterism opens the heart and the mind of sincere Christians to appreciate so many, many areas of how the whole Bible is an amazing covenantal communication, with language that progressively harmonizes with itself from the Book of Genesis to the final Come Lord Jesus. To disagree is okay, but reject is harmful.

DANIEL AND THE LAST DAYS

One of my favorite childhood songs was called "Dare to Be A Daniel". I remember the following lyrics, "Dare to be a Daniel. Dare to stand alone. Dare to have a purpose firm. Dare to make it known." The song is based upon the steady strong character traits of the ancient Hebrew Prophet Daniel, who was taken to Babylon under the rulership of Nebuchadnezzar. There Daniel was raised up by Yahweh to be a solidly decent Jew in his captivity who never compromised his adoration for his God, yet also never failed to be a principled and faithful servant of a pagan king! Daniel walked in his integrity without the camera, lights and action. He prayed faithfully every day toward Jerusalem, ate his kosher diet, and still managed to provide necessary help to the king who was troubled by his dreams. God permitted Daniel to interpret the king's dreams accurately and thus prove his trustworthiness. Daniel is a great model of faithfulness!

Powerful political types in the kingdom were extremely jealous of Daniel. They saw that he was trusted by the king and they hated his guts for it. They plotted to have him thrown into a lion's den under the King Darius later in his career. God prevented Daniel from being lunch for the hungry lions and turned the tables on those who hated him. Daniel never whined nor complained but was steadfast, both when he was in a position of authority, and during the occasion when he was unjustly accused by enemies. So it is that many Christians, including me, grew up loving a song about the goal of emulating Daniel in life.

Daniel was given distinct revelations about the end of his ethnic people. In the ninth chapter of the Book of Daniel, the prophet was told that seventy weeks were determined for his people, the Jews. The revelation further explained to Daniel that these seventy weeks were seventy weeks of years, meaning that a little more than 490 years from the time he received this word from God, his people would experience their last days. The temple would be rebuilt in his homeland, (which Daniel would not be able to live to see), and a great time would end the nation like a flood. Such is what occurred in the war between Rome and Jerusalem. The timing is absolutely amazing, so much so that unbelieving scholars have to do some magic with history to avoid the obvious strong evidence for supernatural guidance to this ancient prophet! Included in the seventy weeks is the prophecy of Messiah Who establishes righteousness, Who is cut off, and of the prince that destroys the temple in Jerusalem. History verifies the fulfillment of this prophecy.

Jesus spoke of the prophecy of Daniel as a reference point for the war between Rome and Jerusalem when He told His disciples, as recorded in Matthew 24, Mark 13, and Luke 21, about the pending devastating abomination that would leave Jerusalem desolate. As history records, the Romans destroyed the City and the Temple, sold the survivors into slavery and the world of the Old Covenant physical temple worship system, the center of Jewish life, ended as Daniel was allowed to foresee many centuries before. Jesus said that the prophecy given to Daniel would occur and history says that it did. The last days came to pass as Daniel foresaw and as our Lord foretold in the First Century.

Dare to be a Daniel. It does seem like the Christian who is willing to accept fulfilled prophecy and to cease looking for God to fulfill it again in modern times is called upon to be like Daniel. The temptation for preachers and teachers who want to avoid being marginalized in the book and movie market of the day is to ignore Daniel's seventy weeks, and to ignore our Lord Jesus Christ applying those prophecies to the destruction of First Century Jerusalem. Why is it so difficult for believers living in the Twenty-First Century to acknowledge that the last days have been completed? There are many, but most of the reasons are that too many ordinary literate Christians are afraid to question the expertise of theological gurus who have an axe to grind. The fact is that it is not easy to be a Christian Daniel and stand for the truth when there is a major social price to pay among the fellowship of believers. But, that is the call of Christ.

FIRST CORINTHIANS FIFTEEN AND THE RESURRECTION OF CHRISTIANS

One of the areas of major dispute with the fact that the last days have been already completely fulfilled in the First Century is the question marks that arise about the resurrection of Christians who have passed into the eternal joy. Many of us have been trained to expect that some kind of visible emergence from the graveyards of all places where natural decaying bodies are is necessary in order to believe that Christ has raised the dead. But, does that fit with what the Apostle Paul taught the believers in First Century Corinth? Does the Apostle actually teach that decayed bodies must be made physically alive again?

The fifteenth chapter of the Apostle Paul's first letter to Christians living in First Century Corinth is a major teaching on the nature of the resurrection. In it, the Apostle rebukes those who deny the fact that God raises the dead. The raising of the dead is the Christian hope as well as the long expected hope of the Old Covenant Jewish people. They shared the hope that the dead would come to life, and this is addressed throughout this chapter. The resurrection and immortality of the Christian is a wonderful Bible truth!

What is particularly interesting is the distinction that the Apostle makes between a natural body and a spiritual body. By calling the eternal body "spiritual", this is not to undermine the reality of its practical functioning as a real body. But, the distinction is noted that a natural body is placed into the grave, and a spiritual body emerges. What is that saying? At minimum, it seems to be saying that there is no reason for anyone to expect that the bodies of the Christians who fell asleep in Jesus during the time when the Apostles were preaching and teaching were going to visibly arise. Unlike our Lord's body, there is no promise given to Christian believers that our bodies would not decay! To expect that there should have been a visible emergence of dead bodies from everywhere that Christians had died during that time is to flatly contradict what the Apostle goes to lengths to explain very clearly. The body that emerges from the grave is NOT the same physical and natural body that was placed into the grave.

There are all kinds of disputes about the nature of the Christian's raising up from out among the dead. There are Christians who do not see the event as individual Christians taking on new bodies, but most Christians believe it is about each individual Christian receiving a new body. Either way, there is no necessity in the language of the fifteenth chapter of the Book of First Corinthians, which is the main teaching about the nature of the raising of believers from the dead, for decayed bodies used for the necessities of living in the life of earth, to be revived before putting on immortality!

Immortality is the gift that God has guaranteed in Jesus Christ to all who are believers in His Son Jesus Christ, and who have called upon the name of Jesus Christ. This precious gift does not at all require that the mortal remains come back to life. It is nearly impossible to set aside traditional concepts about such things, but it must be noted that our temptation to demand that the dead bodies of Christians be resuscitated is not a teaching that fits with the most detailed description of the Christian's raising from the dead that we are given by the Apostles! It is perfectly compatible with what the Holy Spirit teaches through the Apostle Paul for the dead in Christ who emptied the realm of the dead in 70 A.D. to have their new eternal bodies and for all who die in the Lord since then to automatically receive their new body. The bodily resurrection of the Christian does not depend upon the bodies we leave behind.

The book '*LOVE GOD AND LEAVE THE LAST DAYS BEHIND*' challenges the hugely popular giants of religion who, like the medieval opposition to the facts of the orbit of the earth around the sun, deny the coming of the Son of Man as ending the Biblical last days in the 1ˢᵗ Century A.D. The implications of admitting the truth are enormous for all areas of life, including the credibility of Jesus and His Apostles, as well as the energy to quit getting high on sensationalism about 666 on much of the Christian Right, or selling out to socialism and new age hollywood liberalism on the Christian Left. Both sides will be revitalized to build a better future for our kids because we fully expect the world to continue. The last days are behind us!

SUMMARY OF LOVE GOD AND LEAVE THE LAST DAYS BEHIND

It was a delight to visit with a Christian brother who serves a local parish as their senior congregational leader. He is also a candidate for a doctorate. In the course of our visit at Starbuck's, I brought up the subject of this book. As we discussed the general idea of how the plan of God for the ages is to unfold, and the specific proposition of my book that the biblical last days ended in the First Century A.D., he began to raise question after question. It was an intriguing discussion because it compelled one more question. This reminded me why I wanted to write this book in the first place. When I became firmly convinced many years ago that certain Bible passages were saying what they appear to be saying that indicate so plainly that the coming of the Lord was going to happen real soon to those persons living at that time, it started in my mind a series of questions, each followed up by more questions. It has that powerful effect, I think, on many Christians who realize just how many aspects of how we have understood the overall teaching of the Bible is effected by this one change in our view.

The commonsense question for all of us to ask when we think about the subject of the biblical last days is simply "the last days of what?" It certainly could not have meant the last days of world history. Last days of anything do not last for nearly two thousand years. That's ridiculous. It was plainly the first days of the New Covenant kingdom. Jesus rose again and ascended into the heavens, as we read about in Acts chapter 1, and began to reign over heaven and earth. There was an overlap between the kingdom of God with Christ now reigning as the crucified and risen King, and the Old

Covenant establishment of animal sacrifices and various important Jewish temple and synagogue customs as the prescribed way of Yahweh. For about forty years, the kingdom of God in the form of Messiah working from heaven with His holy Apostles to plant the Good News among the nations was in conflict with the Jewish rulers who did not want an end to the Temple system, which was their livelihood and source of power. The rulers were more than willing to cooperate with the powers of Caesar through the mighty Roman Empire to preserve their own high positions, which were threatened by the existence of Jewish Christians.

This showdown was going to prove to be the last days of the little growing Jesus is Messiah Movement, or else, it was going to be the last days of the physical temple system centered in physical Jerusalem. One or the other was about to emerge as God's true Israel forever from the events of the Apostolic Age of transition between Christ ascending to His reign until His coming to judge First Century Jerusalem with the armies of Rome. That Rome and Jerusalem turned against each other, after decades of cooperating to persecute and prosecute the people of Messiah Jesus, is a major development leading up to the war that finally destroyed the temple and the City of Jerusalem, and led the survivors into slavery. The last days, then, have been traditionally understood by most Christians as something that is utterly disconnected from the destruction of the temple. I grew up never hearing about the destruction of Jerusalem at all in church Bible classes. Why is that? Jesus foretold the destruction of Jerusalem and history affirms that Christ's words came to pass. Why, then, do so many Christians hate the subject of a fulfilled prophetic miracle? Part of the reason I wrote this book is to help answer that question.

ABOUT THE WRITER AND THE SUBCULTURE OF MANY RELIGIOUS POOR PEOPLE

Paul Richard Strange, Sr. was born January 20, 1954 to William and Una Strange in Osborn, Kansas. He was the 7th of nine children born to this union. Also, his oldest brother, who was in the Air Force when he was born, came from a previous marriage of William Strange, so there were ten altogether. They were poor. During his childhood, Paul lived in a number of places, but mostly Topeka until age twelve, and then, Salina until after his first marriage at age 19. He enlisted in the Navy from Abilene, and served in San Diego as a hospital corpsman during his first four year tour. There was a break in service, when he relocated to Wichita, Kansas, where this marriage ended in divorce in 1978. Paul signed up for another four years and was assigned to the Naval Hospital, Whidbey Island in Oak Harbor, Washington.

Here Paul attended Family Bible Church of Oak Harbor. He married Jacquelyn "A" Dougherty. (Her middle initial was her birth middle name, which gave him the right in his mind to change her middle name to "Angel"). They enjoyed living in Washington State during this time as a Navy family.

Paul is the proud dad of five children: Timothy, Priscilla, Stefanie, Paul Jr., and Luke. He has a son by marriage, Justin Hentschel who is married to Stefanie. He has three daughters by marriage, Michelle, Jessica, and Kristen, married to Timothy, Paul Jr., and Luke, respectively. His fourteen grandkids are Dominic, Teirra, Neveah, Gabrielle, Kenneth, Matthew, Paul III, Gracie, Isabel, Samantha, Rebekah, Rylee, Emily, and Micah. Paul's post-military career was serving veterans in the VA Hospital System.

Paul grew up in a home where love for God and the Bible was encouraged. There were diverse church and spiritual influences, as well as trends which seemed to contradict the values of the Bible and the Church. Nevertheless, from early years and throughout life, Paul was always convinced that God Is and that the Bible is given by inspiration of God, even during seasons in life of not being certain where he stood with God personally. Doctrinal differences among the church groups his family were exposed to, as well as many family conversations about various religious subjects, produced a desire to study what the Bible actually says as independently as possible. Thus, he began to read the Bible early in life, often not being sure of understanding the Bible well, but confident that it offered real answers to life, anyway.

Most of his adult life was spent as a member of non-denominational Bible churches, and he loved to listen to 'Thru the Bible Radio' with Dr. J. Vernon McGee. The majority of pastors of Bible churches were taught and believe in what is called "dispensational premillennialism", which was made famous by the Schofield Bible early in the Twentieth Century. Later, the popular version became wildly popular in the 1970's through the best-seller 'The Late Great Planet Earth', written by Hal Lindsey, a graduate of Dallas Theological Seminary. In the 1990's, this view was again popularized by the novel series "Left Behind", written by Pastor Dr. Tim LaHaye and Jerry Jordan. By the mid-1980's, Paul no longer agreed with this view, which was still extremely popular, almost a dogma, among many, many American Evangelicals.

Reading the little book "The Great Tribulation" by David Chilton was one of many change influences at this time. Paul had been unable to accept the general answers that the leaders in Bible churches would offer to questions about why Jesus said, "this generation shall not pass away until all these things are fulfilled", when Jesus explained the time of the end to His disciples on the Mount of Olives. His journey into accepting that the last days are behind is what this book is about. The fact that the last days ended in the events of the 1st Century is still treated skeptically by most Bible scholars, in spite of providing clarity, consistency, and reasonable, as well as coherent understanding of Bible passages about Bible prophecy. One of Paul's special privileges in life was serving two Presbyterian churches as a layman supply pastor while considering the possibility of ordination. This aided him to try to be concise with language. Hopefully, this book will challenge many to place Christ above all else in pursuit of Bible truth.

CPSIA information can be obtained
at www.ICGtesting.com
Printed in the USA
LVHW100921310123
738033LV00004B/2

9 798886 228458